COMPANIES AND MEN

Business Enterprise in America

This is a volume in the Arno Press collection

COMPANIES AND MEN
Business Enterprise in America

Advisory Editors
STUART BRUCHEY
VINCENT P. CAROSSO

*See last pages of this volume
for a complete list of titles*

⌐ A HISTORY
OF PROFESSIONAL MANAGEMENT
IN AMERICAN INDUSTRY ⌐

Hayward Janes Holbert

ARNO PRESS
A New York Times Company
1976

Editorial Supervision: ANDREA HICKS

———◆———

First publication in book form, Arno Press, 1976

COMPANIES AND MEN: Business Enterprise in America
ISBN for complete set: 0-405-08062-X
See last pages of this volume for titles.

Manufactured in the United States of America

———◆———

Library of Congress Cataloging in Publication Data

Holbert, Hayward Janes.
   A history of professional management in American
industry.

   (Companies and men, business enterprise in America)
   Reprint of the author's thesis, New York University,
1940.
   1. Industrial management--United States--History.
I. Title. II. Series.
HD30.5.H64 1976   658.4'00973   75-41761
ISBN 0-405-08077-8

A HISTORY OF PROFESSIONAL MANAGEMENT IN AMERICAN INDUSTRY

HAYWARD JAMES HOLBERT

Submitted in partial fulfillment of the
requirements for the degree of Doctor of
Philosophy in the School of Education of
New York University

1940

TABLE OF CONTENTS

CHAPTER I
INTRODUCTION

This study will be an attempt to follow the period from the beginning of the industrial era to the present time, tracing the growth of management in industry from the early units with all functions concentrated in a single individual to the present highly complex types of organization.

The importance of management has greatly increased since the Civil War. Before that time, management was guided by personal judgment and "rule of thumb" methods in its conduct of business. As the size of the individual enterprise increased, the problems of management became more complex, which resulted in the development of men who made it their life work to submit these problems to study and analysis.

These pioneers were technically trained men who brought an analytical approach to the problem. It may seem, during this phase, that too much attention has been given to Frederick W. Taylor, but his work is known and recognized in every country in the world touched by the problems of mechanized industry. It was through the development of his underlying philosophy, that the United States achieved its pre-eminence in the management field.

From approximately the turn of the century, rapid advances in technological improvements forced a corresponding change in managerial practices. The increase in size and complexity of the industrial unit, due to the mechanization of industry, caused management to take stock of itself. As a result of this inventory, management realized that the

advent of the machine had not only completely changed production, but
in doing so had evolved a new philosophy in accounting, supervision,
and management.

After the World War management began to move rapidly towards
more scientific methods of investigation, the elimination of waste,
and the setting up of improved standards.

By a study of the available sources an attempt will be made to
answer the following questions: (1) What has been the history of industrial management in the United States? (2) Does the historical
background developed by the investigation reveal one or more groups of
individuals who have conducted themselves as if management were a profession? (3) Do the trends and tendencies discernible from the historical data show evidence that management is becoming a professional occupation? (4) What are the qualifications in education and experience for
those intending management as a career?

The term "scientific management" has been used throughout the
study because of its universal acceptance in modern business practice.

Oliver Sheldon in his "Philosophy of Management" says on this
subject: "The science of management has not yet been reduced to an ac-
ceptable form. . . . in practicing the art of management, we are working
upon a partially scientific and partially unscientific basis. The efforts of those who are furthering the cause of 'scientific management'
are directed, therefore, to rendering that basis increasingly scientific,
so that the exercise of management may be based upon a wider span of
knowledge. . . . The practice of management is, therefore, not a science,
but the human application of a science. Indeed, were management a
science alone, it could have no human philosophy."[1]

1. O. Sheldon, Philosophy of Management, p. 176.

E. D. Jones uses this definition: "Scientific management may be defined and described somewhat as follows: It is a body of rules, together with their appropriate expression in physical and administrative mechanism and specialized executives, to be operated coordinately as a system for the achievement of a new strictness in control of the processes of production. As this system invites the cooperation of the workmen, it develops a further exact and refined technique for the analysis of human operations and the synthesis of the elements into standard tasks, together with a system of rewards based upon individual performance."[1]

Chronologically, the investigation covers the period from the rapid industrial growth in the United States up to the present time. The period prior to 1870 has been investigated only to the extent that it will help us to understand conditions and developments thereafter.

Geographically, the investigation will mainly be confined to industries within the United States. An exception has been made where influences can be directly traced to development abroad. This applies specially to the early beginnings of industry in the United States. These early developments were greatly influenced by theory and practice abroad. In addition, due cognizance is taken of the international aspects of the subject.

The study, for the most part, is restricted to industrial management with particular emphasis on manufacturing industries.

---

1. E. D. Jones, _The Administration of Industrial Enterprises_, pp. 201-202.

ADDENDA TO CHAPTER I

The importance of the history of management has increased ever
since the Civil War. Up to that time, management operated along traditional
lines, using personal judgment and rule-of-thumb methods for the conduct
of business. But as the size of the individual manufacturing enterprise
increased, the problems relating to management, especially internal management, became more complex, and gradually men appeared who made it their duty
and life-work to submit these problems to study and analysis.

This movement was already well under way when, in 1878, Frederick W.
Taylor, then a young man of 22, began to work at the plant of the Midvale
Steel Company in Philadelphia. Taylor was gifted with extraordinary powers
of observation and analysis. His character was exceedingly dynamic and
forceful, yet friendly.

His experiment of laborers loading pig iron into flat-cars, which
trebled their output, has become a classic. It marked the beginning of a
professional attitude towards management problems in industry. Taylor was
able to accomplish this remarkable improvement by close study of methods
resulting in reduced fatigue, and by adopting a schedule of payment resulting in increa ed wages for the men. Along with this went the development
of a friendly, and cooperative supervision; he willingly and ably shouldered
those responsibilities which management is far better qualified to assume
than the workman.

During these early beginnings Taylor acquired a group of ardent
followers, both in the United States and in Europe. This group increased
slowly but steadily, and each member contributed something of his own to the

new science.

Public attention was first focused toward this new science during the Eastern Rate Case Hearings in 1910 and 1911. At that time, Louis D. Brandeis, later a justice of the Supreme Court, represented a group of shippers who opposed an increase in railroad rates at the hearings held by the Interstate Commerce Commission. Brandeis created a nation-wide sensation when he introduced the testimony of several engineers and experts to show that the proposed increases were necessitated by inefficient management of the railroads.

Today, indications are that management may possibly take its place among the recognised professions in the not too distant future. We find many examples of this new conception on management. In 1925, Lucius R. Eastman, President of the Hills Brothers Company, and also President of the Merchants' Association of New York, made the following statement on the application of the scientific method to business:

> "No longer will the world be satisfied to allow its business affairs to be run in a hit or miss fashion -- meeting the emergency when it comes -- allowing success to be dependent upon lucky guesses -- or allowing a business to be managed by a man of the jungle mind who is controlled by prejudice, by his emotions, by the whims of the moment. It isn't sensible. It is too wasteful.
> "And what do we find taking place? Just as in the professions of the ministry, law and medicine, we developed the special training schools to fit men for their work, so in the last twenty or thirty years we have been developing the schools of business administration. Eventually the influence of these schools is bound to have a tremendous effect on business generally." [1]

The early beginnings of the management movement have been traced and the important events up to the present. The development of groups have indicated that they conduct themselves and their individual and group activities in a manner which leads to the conclusion that management is

---

1. Lucius R. Eastman, "The Future of the Business Man." An address held at the A.M.A. Annual Meeting in New York in 1925. American Management Association; Annual Convention Series No. 12; New York, 1925, p. 6.

regarded by them as a profession. Present tendencies point even more clearly in that direction.

In discussing the qualification in education, it must be recognized that management is in part a science and in part an art; training must, therefore, be in both. This point has been given special consideration in the last chapter of the study. Education must, no doubt, be along lines of personnel problems of leadership, supervision, and training of subordinates.[1] For functional management, a training of a general and vocational character is needed. Functional officers are highly specialized and have technical abilities which cannot be picked up in a haphazard manner. These activities focus around the executive; the latter must, therefore, understand and be able to appreciate the work these functional men are doing. From these requirements a comprehensive program of education in the science of management can be deduced; it will be a course in subjects immediately concerned with management, and in addition, some technical training along lines which the particular manufacturing establishment may call for.[2]

The history of the industrial and economic development of the United States shows an increasing number of large and complicated organizational structures. Accompanying this growth are economic factors and social influences, all tending to increase the number of employees and to widen the distribution of ownership in the individual industrial enterprise. This industrial expansion has required management of progressively greater organizing ability throughout, and management of increasing specialized ability in each department and subdivision of industrial activity.

---

1. See also: Harold B. Bergen and Garrett Lawrence Bergen: "Executive Training Programs"; American Management Association, General Management Series, No. 107, 1929, pp. 1-32
2. See also: Oliver Sheldon: "The Philosophy of Management"; New York, 1924; particularly the chapter on "Training for Industrial Management, pp. 248-279.

This history should act as a guide to students and to those engaged in management, as it will enable them to view present conditions in their proper perspective. It should also aid them in planning their personal programs of training and education. No such treatment of the subject is yet available.

Employers will find such a study a practical aid in guiding them in the selection of those who will comprise the management group.

Schools of business (both secondary and in higher education) will find such a study of value as a guide in preparing present curricula and in planning for future trends in business education.

Continued research and engineering developments will undoubtedly result in new products and new processes more complex in their nature than any now existing. There has been, and will be, a corresponding need for more able management, better trained and equipped to control and direct the increasingly numerous and diversified activities of industrial organisations of the future.

From a broad viewpoint and a general knowledge of the subject, there appears to be a tendency for management to become a recognised profession which will include many highly specialised branches. A verification or disproval of this hypothesis must necessarily rely upon a comparative historical study.

Chronologically, the investigation covers the period from the rapid industrial growth in the United States up to the present time. The period prior to 1850 has been investigated only to the extent as it will help us to understand conditions and developments after 1850.

Geographically, the investigation will mainly be confined, and is mainly confined to industries within the United States. An exception has been made where influences can be directly traced to some development abroad.

This applies specially to the early beginnings of industry in the United States. These early developments were greatly influenced by theory and practice abroad.

The study excludes for the most part all management of a governmental or military nature, and is restricted to industrial management with particular emphasis on manufacturing industries.

Webster's New International Dictionary (G. C. Merriam Company, Springfield, Massachusetts, 1933) gives the following definitions:

Profession: "3. That of which one professes knowledge, the occupation, if not purely commercial, mechanical, agricultural, and the like, to which one devotes one's self; a calling in which one professes to have acquired some special knowledge used by way either of instructing, guiding, or advising others or serving them in some art, etc.

"4. The collective body of persons engaged in a calling, etc."

Professional: "1. Of or pertaining to a profession or calling; conforming to the rules or standards of a profession; following a profession, or some line of conduct as if it were a profession, etc."

Management: "Act or art of managing; the manner of treating, directing, carrying on, or using for a purpose; conduct, administration, guidance, control, etc."

In measuring the development of professional management, two elements are necessary. The first of these is that the measure must be as objective as possible. The second requirement is that the quality of being professional be adequately determined. This has been done:
A. By referring professional to its development in connection with science in accordance with encyclopedia definition.

v

1. Is there an orderly accumulation of knowledge?

2. Is there a development of methods characteristic of that discipline?

B. The development of professional management has also been traced by referring professional in accordance with encyclopedia definition to its development and use in the world of sports where the criteria is payment of money
and the development of a standard of ethics.

At the Thirtieth Annual Congress of Medical Education, Licensure
and Hospitals, in Chicago, on February 12, 1937, Dean Justin Miller said,
"The purpose of professional licensure is fundamentally to secure to society
the benefits which come from the services of a highly skilled group and to
protect society from those who are not highly skilled, yet profess to be, or
from those who, being hi hly skilled, are nevertheless so unprincipled as to
misuse their superior knowledge to the disadvantage of the people." [1]

The standards finally adopted will show whether they are so low
that the profession will be obliged to constantly eliminate its shyster or,
so high that the profession will be constantly concerned with activities from
the outside; in either case, the application to management has its limitation
in this respect since the individual has to prove his ability in a very practical manner, and, success or failure will finally determine his place.

For a philosophy of management we may again use Dean Justin Miller's
definition, which reads as follows:

> "In more general application and usually with 'the' or 'a'
> philosophy denotes a systematic body of general conceptions, or-
> dinarily with the impli ation of their practical application." [2]

"Professional licensure", said Dean Justin Miller, "calls for a
minimum of achievement which may be deemed adequate to guarantee safe

---

1. Justin Miller: "The Philosophy of Professional Licensure"; an address at
    the National Council of State Boards of Engineer Examiners; Columbia,
    S. C., 1937, p. 2
2 Ibid.

performance within the field of practice. This is also true in the case of management. Hence it means possibilities of achievement in the future; one of the essential elements in the definition of the word license is that it is ACTION, authority or liberty to do or forebear any act; a proper permission from the AUTHORITY to PERFORM certain acts, or to carry on a certain business which without such permission would be illegal as a license to preach, to practice medicine, to sell gunpowder, etc." [1]

"So far as a license to carry on business is concerned, nothing more is required than perfunctory service and the collection of money therefor. But in the case of a profession more is required, we must discover those characteristics of the philosophy of professional (licensure) which distinguish it from ordinary business or other licensure." [2]

The factors to be taken into consideration, according to Dean Justin Miller, are: "(1) The nature of the authority which licenses or authorizes action; (2) The purpose sought to be accomplished by the licensing authority; (3) The nature of the act to be performed; (4) The character, training, and skill required for the proper performance of the act." [3]

Further, in a professional group only members of each group are qualified to set standards and give examinations.

While in business we have the maxim of the law: "Let the buyer beware"; in a profession, on the other hand, we look towards the highest degree of service, and the fullest measure of protection. Hence, the above maxim would not apply because the member of a profession is assumed to be better informed than his client.

---

1. Ibid., pp. 2-3.
2. Ibid., p. 3
3. Ibidem

The lawyer deals with rights, he is an officer of the court and is involved in the functions of Government. A breach of legal ethics defies justice. An engineer is a servant of economics and business; he is involved in commercial cost. A breach of ethics on his part involves the purse and is difficult to conceal. Very similar to this is the profession of management. It is concerned with the proper conduct of business. Business itself is carried on for profits and a breach of ethics will turn those profits into losses; this, too, affects the purse. But while the engineer serves business and economics, management serves economics and the community on a much wider scale. Management may be able to conceal a breach of ethics for a considerable period, but once it becomes public, the whole world will know about it. By that time, it will not only affect the purse of a few, but that of a large number of the community, of business in general, the investors and the working men.

Management has grown in importance both as to personal skill and with respect to the effect of success or failure involved. The advancement of the world during the last 100 years is primarily and pre-eminently due to the growth in manufacturing which in turn was only possible through the continued advancements in the science and the art of management. In its higher branches it is, therefore, a science, and one of the principal sciences for that matter. Pure science is not concerned with financial matters, but already here we have to make an exception in the case of political science. Management, on the other hand, is directly concerned with finance and economics the manager is the practical man among the scientists.

The technical training now given involves a great deal of pure science and it is, therefore, evident that management (or, the manager) should have a comprehensive knowledge of all leading sciences.

CHAPTER II

THE PERIOD BEFORE 1870

Although the ideas of modern management were not applied in the
United States until well after the Civil War, there had been a number
of individuals who had been concerned with the organization of industry
and its more effective control. In 1776, Adam Smith published his
"Wealth of Nations" in which the principle of division of labor was
first clearly laid down. In 1832, a more definite step forward was
made with the advent of Charles Babbage's volume entitled, "On the Economy of Machinery and Manufactures."

A discussion of early problems in management would, therefore,
not be complete without considering Babbage's observations and remarks,
and, in treating this period, free use of this valuable source of information will be made.

To indicate how advanced Babbage was in his ideas, it is obvious
from a study of his works that half a century before, he had envisaged
the central point of Taylor's approach to the problem of management.

With the advancement in manufacturing and the increase in size
of the individual factory, the need for some control became apparent;
the time had passed when a single proprietor was able to supervise his
whole working force. It is, therefore, only natural that attention
should be given to finding some substitute for personal supervision.

Research in some of the earlier writings on the subject reveal
that a few men were becoming aware of factors in modern management
practice, such as: division of labor, wages, cost of materials, profits

to ownership, profits to labor, bonus systems, etc.

In his "Wealth of Nations", Adam Smith begins with the division of labor as the means for increasing its productiveness. "The greatest improvement in the productive powers of labor, and the greater part of the skill, dexterity, and judgment with which it is anywhere directed, or applied, seem to have been the effects of the division of labor." It is, therefore, not surprising to find more and more interest centered around the subject of increasing production through the division of labor.

No doubt, the value of perfecting tools and machinery was greatly enhanced through the application of the principle of division of labor. Improvement in tools helped in this division, and increased the speed of the work. Babbage, in this connection, gives an account of cutting metals, a study which Taylor, more than fifty years later, took as a basis for the foundation of scientific management. Quoting from Babbage: "When each process, by which any article is produced, is the sole occupation of one individual, his whole being devoted to a very limited and simple operation, improvements in the form of his tools, or in the mode of using them, are much more likely to occur to his mind, than if it were distracted by a greater variety of circumstances. Such an improvement in tools is generally the first step in developing a machine. If a piece of metal is to be cut in a lathe, for example, there is one particular angle at which the cutting tool must be held to insure the cleanest cut; and it is quite natural that the idea of fixing the tool at that angle should present itself to an intelligent workman. The necessity of moving the tool slowly and in a direction parallel to itself, would suggest the use of a screw, and thus arises the sliding-rest. When each process has been reduced to some simple tool, the union of all these tools, actuated

by a moving power, constitutes a machine."[1] Of course, a general
knowledge of machinery, and the ability to make drawings are necessary.

The principle of the division of labor is not limited to manual
labor. During the French Revolution the decimal system had been adopted,
and to make its practical application easier, a series of mathematical
tables had to be evolved. The government called upon France's most
distinguished philosophers and mathematicians. By applying the principle of the division of labor, the task was accomplished in a short time.
M. Prony, to whom the task had been assigned, felt helpless with respect
to an approach to the situation. He was especially worried about the
making of the logarithmic tables. Passing before a bookseller's window,
he noticed a copy of Adam Smith's "Wealth of Nations". He opened the
book, and his eyes fell on the chapter, "Of The Division Of Labour". This
gave him the idea of developing his logarithmic tables.

He began by dividing the tremendous task into three sections: the
first section contained only simple numerical calculations to make; the
second section consisted of seven or eight persons acquainted with the
intricacies of mathematics, and they made the formulae; the third section,
consisting of sixty to eighty men, received the orders and the necessary
numbers from the second section, and by simple additions and subtractions,
finished the tables which they then returned to the second section.

Such division presupposes a rather advanced stage of management.
Success depended not only on the division of labor as such; but equally
important in order to profit to the fullest extent from such division,
the proper number of men had to be assigned to each division. This
envisioned Taylor's method of assigning the right task to the right man
sixty years later.

---

1. Charles Babbage, <u>On the Economy of Machinery and Manufactures</u>, pp. 170-171.

Before the use of steam power, investigations and tests were made on the subject of how to conserve man power. Bedelet, a Frenchman, in his "L'Art de Batir" gives an example of such a test. A stone weighing 1,080 pounds, dragged over the floor of the quarry required a force equal to 758 lbs. The same stone dragged over a floor of planks required a force equal to 606 lbs.; after soaping the surfaces of the wood, it required a force equal to 182 lbs.; when the stone was placed on a wooden platform and rollers placed between that and a plank floor, moving the stone required a force of only 22 lbs.

Babbage describes the making of pins by a machine invented in the United States, and he makes comparisons on the advantages of this machine on the following points: (1) The defects to which pins so made are liable. (2) Their advantages, if any, over those made in the usual way. (3) The prime cost of the machine for making the pins. (4) The expense of keeping the machine in repair. (5) The expense of moving the machine and attending to it.[1]

He approaches scientific management when he describes methods for making observations in a factory. Every observation should be put in writing and for each process Babbage suggests the following form for use:

Process ( ) Manufacture ( ) Place ( ) Date ( )

The mode of executing it, with sketches of the tools or

machines, if necessary:..................

The number of persons necessary to attend the machine ( ).

Are the operatives men ( ), women ( ), or children ( )?

If mixed, what are the proportions?

What is the pay of each? (s. d.) (s. d.) (s. d.)

per..........

---

1. Charles Babbage, On the Economy of Machinery and Manufactures, p. 186.

What number of hours ( ) do they work per day?

Is it usual or necessary to work night and day without stopping?

Is the labour performed by piece or day work?

Who provides the tools? Master or men?

Who repair (sic) tools? Master or men?

What degree of skill is required, and how many years apprenticeship? ( )

The number of times the operation is repeated per day or per
hour? ( )

The number of failures ( ) in a thousand?

Whether the workmen or master loses by broken or damaged articles?

If a process is repeated several times, state the loss or increase
of measure, and the loss, if any, at each repetition. ( )[1]

Babbage refers to previous time studies made in France. Couloub[2] in his "Memoires"[3] warns against quick observations. The time should be measured over various days, and at times when the workers are not aware of the fact that they are being observed. He warns especially, "We can hardly warn enough against the risk of mistaken calculation, either as to the speed, or the time it takes to do a certain work, if we make our observation only during a few minutes." Babbage, in referring to time study, asks that care be taken in writing down the time, "for instance, if the observer stands with his watch in his hand before a person heading a pin, the workmen will almost certainly increase his speed, and the

1. Charles Babbage, op. cit., pp. 114-115.
2. Charles Augustus Coulomb, 1753-1806 A.D.
3. Papers published. Vol. 2 of a "Collection de mémoires", made by
     the "Société Francaise de Physique", and published in 1884.
     Paris, France.

estimate will be too large. A much better average will result from
inquiring what quantity will be a fair day's work. When this cannot
be ascertained, the number of operations performed in a given time
may frequently be counted when the workman is quite unconscious that
any person is observing him."[1] He advocates then the counting of the
number of strokes per minute, for instance, of a loom. This could be
done from outside the building, without being seen by the workman.

Aside from time study, fatigue study had already received some
attention. It was known that motions, often repeated, would tire the
laborer much more than diversified work.

In 1817 Ricardo published his chief work "On the Principles of
Political Economy and Taxation". He set up his "Iron Law of Wages"
which had been formulated a few years earlier (1815) by Torrens. During
the early period of industrialism labor was a commodity, and there were
few restrictions, if any, as to the hours of labor, or wages paid. Supply and demand was the dominant factor. Wages for the unskilled were
very low; skilled labor, however, received fair pay. This was especially
true of those qualified to operate the new machines. On the whole,
labor seemed to have been cheap; the early time studies mentioned before
were made for the purpose of determining cost, but the cost of machinery
and raw materials was of greater importance than that of labor. The
situation was better in the large cities where labor societies existed.
Associations of masters of the same trade, or of manufacturers, came
into existence before those of the workmen.

Babbage advocates agreements between these two parties for the
following reasons: to estimate the proportional value of different
kinds of work executed in their trade, for time saving and prevention
of disputes, and also to help in obtaining statistical information either
for private, or for government agencies.[2]

---

1. Charles Babbage, op. cit., pp. 115-116.
2. Ibid., pp. 299-301.

The cost of labor is also affected by division of labor. Division of labor makes it possible to purchase and apply to each process just that quantity of skill and knowledge that is required. This factor was recognized long before 1870, and was applied to both mechanical and mental operations.

The organization of labor had made advances primarily in cities, and manufacturers had made some efforts to remove their grievances; on the other hand, excessive demands by labor were often met by moving factories to other places. In fact, a manufacturer from Glasgow was so discouraged by the conduct of his workmen that he moved to the State of New York.[1]

There is little information available as to the specific treatment of cost of raw materials. Statistics and research on the prices of raw materials, especially metals, however, were made at an early date. A complete study on the cost of the metals had been made in France around 1828, by Heron de Villefosse, and the results of his research was published in "Recherche statistique sur les metaux en France." The volume gives the prices of the metals; and the quantity of finished products resulting from a given quantity of raw material. This points towards cost finding, since studies had been made in comparative costs and prices.

Plant depreciation was not an important factor at this time. The length of service of machinery depends on its perfection, i.e., its original design and construction. However, during this period machinery seldom wore out; new improvements in performance or speed superseded the old machinery long before it wore out.[2]

1. Charles Babbage, On the Economy of Machinery and Manufactures, pp.500-501.
2. Ibid., p. 279.

Division of labor and improved machinery made for cheaper prices, which in turn increased demand, thus partially off-setting the reduction in price. It also made for larger factories. Waste had to be eliminated; this was sometimes accomplished by placing two trades under one roof; one article being manufactured from the waste of the main product.

During the Napoleonic Wars, England was relatively free from competition in manufacturing, which facilitated the great advancement made in the early period of the Industrial Revolution. In the period from 1812 to 1852, however, prices declined from 40 to 80 per cent. This was an incentive for greater efficiency in management. There is no business mortality table available covering this period, but the rate of mortality was, no doubt, great. On the other hand, it caused "management" to make inquiries into the conditions of the market. With this came the need for collecting data on market conditions and prices; thus Sales Analysis had its birth at an early date. Statistical data was gathered in order to determine the additional number of customers which a reduction in price might bring.

Early manufacturing establishments were usually partnerships, in many cases even single ownership. In Great Britain it was only after the repeal of the Bubble Act in 1825, that joint stock companies in the field of manufacturing were formed. But the number of joint stock companies consisted still largely of banks, insurance companies, trading companies, and later the railroads. In manufacturing, the transformation to joint stock companies was slow; the same situation existed in France where single proprietorship was predominant. One of the reasons that may be advanced was the factor of risk involved in manufacturing, and hence the difficulties to obtain capital through the issue of shares.

A characteristic feature of the time was the right to interest which the owner claimed from his capital. His interest might amount to as high as ten per cent of the funds invested in the business, and it was only what was over and above this interest that was considered to be profit. This was in accordance with economic theory which allowed the capitalist first interest on his capital, and then an additional amount, i.e., the profits which accrued to the owner for his taking the risk as entrepreneur. Since interest rates in general were still high, the owner claimed a high rate of interest on his capital. In successful concerns, the profits were usually as high as the interest. Under these circumstances the returns from the business which went to the owner were usually quite satisfactory.

Under such circumstances profits went usually to the ownership of the business with a few exceptions. These exceptions were where the owner had employed a manager on a contractual basis, promising the latter a certain percentage of the profits.

In considering distribution of profits to labor, management is mentioned for a specific reason. Whatever plans were developed and put in operation to give labor a share in the profits were in the first instance, devised to give those who had an influence on profits an additional incentive to increase their efforts. Those who derived benefits from any additions to regular wages were carefully chosen. There were few cases, at first, where all employees were given a share in the profits of the establishment.

Babbage advocates as early as 1832 a system of payment where each one should derive advantage from the success of the whole business. The profits of each individual should advance in the same proportion as the profits of the factory increase. To him, the interest of employer and employee is closely interwoven.

He then goes further and brings a practical example of a method of payment that he had observed in the mines of Cornwall. The benefits derived from the introduction of such a plan are as follows:

(1) Every person employed will benefit directly from the prosperity and success, or else, will be affected by a falling off in his weekly receipts.

(2) Every person employed would have a direct interest in eliminating waste and mismanagement.

(3) The workers' talents would be directed toward improvements in the different departments.

(4) None but workmen of high character and qualifications could obtain admission into such establishments....it would be the common interest of all to admit only the most respectable and skillful.

(5) When any circumstance produced a glut in the market, more skill would be directed to diminishing the cost....

(6) There would be no need for either employers' associations or labor unions, since there would be a most powerful union between employer and employee directly.[1]

The fourth and sixth points mentioned by Babbage are probably close to those for which Taylor stood.

Some form of participation was introduced as early as 1843 in France in a paper manufacturing plant. Later, provisions were made whereby lower paid employees received coupons with which to buy bread whenever its price went above a certain level. Finally in 1847, a plan was drawn up and adopted which would increase production without lowering the quality of the product as often happens in piece-work. Almost all labor was on a piece-work basis. Hence, a plan was drawn up under

---

1. Charles Babbage, "On the Economy of Machinery and Manufactures", pp. 253-254.

which each workman would receive one franc for each thousand kilograms
of product above 25,000 kilograms. This was one of the earlier forms
of bonus payment. Production up to that time had run from 20,000 to
25,000 kilograms per month. It soon increased from 20,000 to 45,000
kilograms, and from 25,000 to 55,000 kilograms respectively, and never
returned to its former level. The resulting increase in wages to the
individual workman was forty per cent. While such an arrangement could
properly be called a bonus plan, Leroy-Beaulieu called it "progressive
wages".[1]

Encouraged through the results thus far obtained, the foreman, and
later the workers who had been with the firm for some years, were allowed a share in the profits of the enterprise. The plan was as
follows:
An employee may invest his savings in the firm and will receive five
per cent on his deposits regardless of the profits of the firm. Once
the amount is above two thousand francs, the deposit is no more regarded
as a savings deposit, but the man becomes a shareholder (commanditaire).
As soon as the sum reaches 100 francs, he is entitled to a share of one
per cent of the "general profits" of the firm. The plan was perfected
after 1860, but since the start was made in 1847, we may consider it
under this period. Savings deposits drew about 12 per cent interest,
of which five per cent represented interest, and the remainder was a
share in the profits of the enterprise. Any amount from 20 francs to
5,000 francs might be deposited. In order to allow stock purchase,
the firm was changed into a corporation and the amount of capital was
increased from its original amount of 3,000,000 francs to 4,500,000
francs.

---

1. Victor Boehmert, Die Gewinnbeteiligung. Untersuchungen ueber
   Arbeitslohn und Unternehmergewinn, Leipzig 1878. 2 vols.

By 1865 the amount of capital belonging to 82 employees was 1,545,000 francs. As regards the savings account, changes were made from time to time with the result that finally each worker had a savings book in which the yearly wages were entered, and at the end of the year the worker was credited with a part of the profits of the firm which was in proportion to his wages. By 1872 the workers' share in the profits was about six per cent of their wages. Employees in more responsible positions received a greater share of the profits. The division of profits between capital and labor, as finally adopted, was as follows: (1) The president of the Board of Managers and the five active managers received their fixed salaries. (2) Five per cent interest is paid on the capital. (3) Each of the six managers (or directors) takes five per cent of the remaining profits. (4) Ten per cent of the profits goes to the superior employees. (5) Twelve per cent goes to the customers of the house. (6) The remainder goes to capital, the participating depositors, and the wage earners of the whole active personnel not admitted to a share in the special profits of any department.

The division of profits was practiced not only on the basis of wages, but also on the basis of the value of the services of the salaried employees, of which the manager retained the right to judge. It also recognized the principles of seniority, and increased the share of the workman in direct proportion to length of service.

In addition to the division of profits as enumerated above, bonuses were paid. Since the work in the different plants of the establishment varied so greatly, different codes were set up. There was a code for glazing, one for finishing, another for the mills, one for the warehouse, etc. The workers in all these divisions received a predetermined share in the special profits of these branches or departments. These profits were based on the profit of the respective department only, and not on the general profits of the business. For this purpose, the net profit of each of these divisions at the end of the year was arrived at, and a special percentage of it was divided among the workers and foremen of the respective departments on the basis of their salaries. In some of the departments the part thus divided amounted to as much as sixty per cent of the profits of the respective department.[1]

As already seen, especially in the case of the bonus payments, production of individual departments increased tremendously. The waste of material, and production costs were considerably decreased. Labor turnover also decreased, and no strikes occurred.

---

1. On Patetorie Cooperative, formerly Laroche-Joubert see:
    A. As primary sources: V. Boehmert, Vol. 1, p. 32, and
       Vol. 2, pp. 212-225; B. Frommer, pp. 93-94.
       As a secondary source: N. P. Gilman, pp. 106-131.

CHAPTER III

DEVELOPMENTS FROM 1870 TO 1900

Early European Labor Experiments.

While labor may be considered a commodity subject to the factors
of supply and demand, management, nevertheless, realized at an early
date its value and superior importance in the whole industrial set-up.
Without labor, machines will not work; without the friendly cooperation
of labor, there will never be a maximum of output.

At a time when our country was in the beginning of a rapid industrial
evolution, in Europe the movement had already grown to the point where
management had to give serious consideration to the problem of labor.

In England, Fawcett writes on the relationship between capital
and labor. He states: "Employers naturally complain that their labourers
feel no concern about their master's interest. Again I repeat that this
must always continue to be the case, whilst employers and employed are
not united by any feelings which arise from a common pecuniary interest."[1]
He tells how employers complain about the inefficiency of labor, and
how they would be glad to pay more if they were only assured that labor
would promote their masters' interest; but it seems to him singular
that employers do not create some common pecuniary interest with labor.
The owner of a business does this when he has a manager on whose activity
the success of the business depends; he stimulates the manager's efforts

---

1. Henry Fawcett, Pauperism, its Causes and Remedies, London and
   New York; 1871, p. 153.

by promising him a share of the aggregate profits realized. Pointing
out the cases already in existence, Fawcett advocates profit-sharing
as the solution to the problem of inefficiency.[1]

In 1871, another volume by Fawcett appeared on "Pauperism, its
Causes and Remedies." Again Fawcett advocates very strongly a co-
partnership between employer and employed. To use his own words:
"All experience shows that there can be no hope of introducing more
harmonious relations, unless employers and employed are both made to
feel that they have an immediate and direct interest in the success
of the work in which they are engaged."[2] In order to be effective,
any extra remuneration must be given in such a way that the laborer
can immediately see cause and effect.[3]

In France the problem of labor was becoming acute. In 1870,
Charles M. Robert wrote a book on "La Suppression des Greves", in which
he strongly advocates giving labor a share in the profits of the enterprise. As a remedy for the situation, he advocated some sort of participation in order to create a common interest between employer and employee.[4]

As a result of a growing resentment to large profits in industry,
Victor Boehmert, professor of economics at the Polytechnikum at Zurich,
and later at Dresden, was asked to give his opinion on the subject. He
was not willing to do so, however, without first making a thorough investigation of the subject. He had started such an investigation while
still in Switzerland, and continued it in Germany, France, England, and
the United States. He sent out questionnaires to well-known firms in
all these countries. The results of his investigation were published

---

1. Henry Fawcett, Op. cit., p. 154.
2. Ibid., p. 164.
3. Ibid., p. 165.
4. Charles Robert: La Suppression des Greves par l'Association aux
        Benefices (conference faite a la Sorbonne le 27 decembre
        1869.) Paris 1870. see pp. 6-9.

in two volumes.[1] Boehmert gathered information on 81 cases which showed participation of labor in one way or another.

The French government appointed a commission in order to make a similar investigation. The commission had twenty-four members, all of whom were high officials of the French government.

In 1878, Frommer subjected the two existing inquiries to a severe test and analysis. Of the cases mentioned by Boehmert, Frommer left out sixty-nine due to lack of information on the actual situation, or because the results obtained were negligible, or where conditions were such that information which had been obtained could not be relied on. He also dropped all cases where labor was simply given some reward in the form of a Christmas or New Year's present which had no relationship to the work performed, the amount of wages, or the kind of work done. He further left out cases of ordinary piece-work, and cases where labor was simply permitted to buy shares on the same basis as the public. The French investigation is even more severely treated by Frommer. He regrets that the committee consisted only of government officials and did not include independent men either from the French Chamber, Senate, or from some University. Another weak point in the French investigation was one of method; the person making the interview had the questions to be asked in printed form before him, and it was conducted behind closed doors, i.e., in meetings at which neither the public nor the press were allowed to be present. Frommer thus states: "The enquete" was mostly a political manouvre in order to show the interest the government has in the working classes, and to show the government's benevolence to them.[2]

1. Victor Boehmert, Die Gewinnbeteiligung. Untersuchungen ueber Arbeitslohn und Unternehmergewinn, Leipzig 1878, 2 Vols.
2. H. Frommer, Gewinnbeteiligung, p. 45.

The cases which shall presently be mentioned have been tested, checked, and analysed by Frommer. They give some insight into the problems confronted by management and how the situation was dealt with in Europe.

In France the firm of Redouly & Cie is cited as being typical. The business had been started on a small scale in 1826, but had steadily increased in size. The corporation had a capital of 400,000 francs. Each of the two directors of the firm had 100,000 francs in the business; the other 200,000 francs belonged to the Mutual Aid Society of the workers of the establishment which had been formed as early as 1838. The two directors were chosen for life by the "noyau" (inner circle) of the workers. If the incoming director had not the necessary cash, his predecessor was to leave his money with the firm until the new director had been able to supply the needed amount. These directors, once elected, had full power to manage the firm as they saw fit.

The "noyau" or inner circle of workers was made up of those who had worked for at least five years for the firm and who were between the ages of 25 and 40, and were directors. Newcomers were elected to membership by those who were already members. The "noyau" in turn elected a board and a committee of conciliation. They were all full time employees, and all were members of the Mutual Aid Society of the firm.

The basis of participation was as follows: The participation in the profits of the company was enlarged to include all working for the firm, i.e., not only the members of the "noyau"; it included everybody whether a permanent worker, a casual hand, or an apprentice. Twenty-five per cent of the net profit went to the directors, another twenty-five per cent to the Mutual Aid Society, and fifty per cent was divided among the workers of the firm (excluding piece-workers). Net profit is the profit left after deducting overhead costs, including the salaries of

the directors, and an interest on the capital of five per cent. A
General Reserve Fund was maintained at 100,000 francs, or one-fourth
the amount of the capital, and was to be replenished whenever it had
been drawn upon. Some of the effects of this arrangement can be seen
from the following table:

Year	Number of those taking part in the division of Profits	Percentage of Annual Wages
1870	758	14%
1871	1,058	12
1872	976	12
1873	655	13
1874	827	13
1875	1,052	14
1876	1,081	16
1877	826	18
1878	1,052	18
1879	1,125	18
1880	949	19
1881	1,125	20
1882	996	22
1883	858	23
1884	824	24 etc.

Results: The profit depended to a great extent upon the quality of the
work, as well as upon the speed with which it was done. The participation
of the workers was very high. It resulted in an increase of work energy
(energy with which the employee did his work); attendance at work became
regular; the employees controlled each other under the system; there
were no labor troubles; the workers behaved properly toward the clientele

because they themselves had an interest in giving satisfaction.[1]

The firm of Billon et Isaac, Geneva, Switzerland, manufactured cases and parts of the mechanism of music boxes, and employed about one hundred workers on the average. The work was done with machinery, but required skilled and semi-skilled labor. The basis for participation was: After necessary provision for amortization and interest on capital at current rates had been made, one half of the remaining profits was to be divided between the managers and the stockholders, and the other half was to go to all workmen employed for three months or more, the amount to be divided in proportion to their wages. This was probably the most generous plan so far devised. Of the employees' share one-half was paid out in cash at the end of the year, while the other half was retained in the firm to be applied toward the purchase of 100 franc shares of the company. Until the amount reached 100 francs, the money bore interest at six per cent. No worker could acquire shares of a value in excess of one-third of his annual wages. Those workers who owned shares were thus able to influence the policy of the firm by sending their representatives. The share thus acquired by the workers could not freely be sold by them, but if the worker left the employ of the firm, they had to be resold to the firm. If a worker left the factory without taking proper leave (two weeks' advance notice) he would lose his share in the profit of the current year, and he lost his participation generally for the last three months during which he was in the firm's employ. An exception to this rule was made in case of sickness, death, or the laying off of labor on account of lack of work.

---

1. B. Frommer, Gewinnbeteiligung, p. 91. See also pp. 87-91.

Under such a generous plan the results were satisfactory to both parties. It created that common pecuniary interest which is so essential to a proper solution of the managerial problem of labor; it is the necessary incentive without which labor will not be spurred to maximum exertion. Applied to the case of Billon et Isaac, labor certainly showed greater willingness to do the best; it was one of the greatest stimuli ever given to employees, and it met with great success. The participation of the workers in percentage to their wages (yearly) was as follows:

1871-2	18½%
1872-3	28½%
1873-4	20½%
1874-5	23½%
1875-6	17%
1876-7	4%
1877-8	none
1878-9	8%
1879-80	10%
1880-1	15%
1881-2	20%
1882-3	18%
1883-4	10%
1884-7	none

In the first year after the plan went into effect, the president of the company was in a position to announce increased dividends to stockholders, so that the plan had cost them nothing, but had even increased their own share in the profits. In addition, it brought about improvements in the products, as well as a lowering of costs, so that the products could be sold more cheaply.

The plan brought about a very friendly relationship between management and labor, and contests and disputes were thus avoided. When the contract ended, the stockholders on the advice of the management, voted to continue the plan.[1]

The system used in the case of Billon et Isaac is probably the best to supplement wages and to make good for unjust situations which may be present in the wage system. It proved to be a greater stimulus than piece-work in that the laborer was not only interested in the quantity, but also in the quality of the work. It was also an inducement for the workers to save regularly.[2]

Cooperation and Participation in the United States.

Since the Industrial Revolution in the United States began at a much later date, the problems were not as pressing as they were during the same period in Europe. It is also interesting to note that strikes were fewer and a better feeling seems to have existed between employer and employed. This may be due to a great extent to the absence of class distinction and class-hatred in our country. In Europe this hatred was deep-rooted and, as we can see from the foregoing, it was only in France that serious attempts on any large scale were made to bridge this antagonism. In the latter country, it was tradition which went as far back as the French Revolution and which resulted in that characteristically paternalistic attitude of the employer toward the employed.

---

1. H. Frommer, pp. 85-87;   Victor Boehmert, Vol. 1, pp. 78-82, and
        pp. 272-297.
2. Ibid. p. 158.

It was not until 1878 that the Order of Sovereigns made an attempt at introducing the "Rochdale plan" of cooperation in this country. This plan was called the National Council of the Order of Sovereigns of Industry and was founded in Springfield, Massachusetts, for the purpose of "organized resistance to the organized encroachment of the monopolies and other evils of the existing industrial and commercial system. It was supposed to help establish a better system of economical exchanges and to promote, on a basis of equity and liberty, mutual fellowship and cooperative action among the producers and consumers of wealth throughout the earth...."[1]

Great efforts were made by the National Council and its lecturer, John Arvis, to spread the knowledge of distributive cooperation. Following is the basis on which nearly half of these stores started and on which nearly all which succeeded were founded:

1. Allow but one vote to a shareholder, without regard to the number of shares held.

2. Shares to draw a minimum rate of interest.

3. Dividends to be made only on purchases, and that quarterly.

4. Every member of the order entitled to full dividends on purchases, provided the directors may retain such dividends at their discretion until the same shall amount to at least one share of stock.

5. Shares not to exceed $5. each, etc.......

Many attempts were made at cooperatives of wage earners in the West, but few of them have succeeded. Some mines were transformed into cooperatives, usually after strikes. During 1873 in Huntsville, Missouri, in one of the largest mines, the miners created a cooperative and paid a royalty to the owners and used the machinery of the old company.

---

1. Edward W. Bemis, History of Cooperation in the United States;
   Johns Hopkins University, Historical and Political Studies,
   Vol. 6, Baltimore 1888, see part on "Cooperation in New
   England."

Companies of a similar nature followed the idea. These companies were: The Cooperative Coal Company of Peoria, Illinois, and The Summit Cooperative Coal & Mining Company of Bevier, Macon County, Missouri.

In the West we find the farmers most active in forming cooperatives. In Ohio a Central Business Agency or Supply House was formed by the State Grange as early as 1876; by 1878 the enterprise had proven itself, and similar cooperatives were founded in Cincinnati and other places. In Ohio and Indiana the formation of cooperative creameries by the farmers proved a success. In Kansas the oldest and most successful of the state's cooperatives was the Johnson County Coop. Association formed in 1876.

In the Atlantic States a few attempts at cooperative manufacturing were tried. One of the most successful was The Cooperative Stove Works at Troy, New York, organized in 1870.

The Cooperative Foundry Company of Rochester, N. Y. was organized in 1867. Its history was somewhat similar to that of the Cooperative Stove Works. In 1885 the Frankford Cooperative Manufacturing Co., Frankford, Pa., was organized with a paid-in capital of $15,000 and beginning with twenty-five employees. In the next year a similar cooperative was formed in Chester, Pa., and in Reading a cooperative cigar manufacturing company was organized around the same time with a capital of $5,000. In New York City the Knights of Labor sponsored several small cooperative manufacturing establishments.

In New England we find that Massachusetts had nine cooperative manufacturing companies by 1875, which had a total capital of $73,250. In 1885, there were ten cooperative factories with a capital of $166,900. While this represents an increase of more than one hundred per cent, it is hardly a significant amount when compared with the increase in size and amount of capital of the non-cooperative manufacturing enterprises.

The same was true in the case of cooperative stores; they increased in size and capital, but not in number. At the time of the study made by Johns Hopkins University (1886) about twenty cooperative stores and associations were listed as then in existence in Massachusetts, the most successful of which was the Danvers Cooperative Union Society in the shoe town of Danvers, Mass.

On the Pacific Coast as well as in the South, the cooperative movement was of little importance, and was usually confined to very small enterprises.

From the foregoing outline on the situation in cooperative enterprise, we can readily see that the movement had but a small foothold in this country. No doubt, the competition of private business seems to have set a limit on the cooperative movement in this country.

Employee Participation in Profit:-

Direct participation as a means of solving the problem of the management of labor has been used very little in the United States. But whatever was done in this direction may properly be regarded as part of the evolution which led to trials in the different types of payment plans for labor and finally culminated in scientific management.

One of the earliest firms which segregated part of its profits for labor, was the A. S. Cameron & Co., Jersey City, N. J., manufacturers of steam pumping machinery. The firm gave its employees ten per cent of the net profits from 1869 to 1877. The profits were divided at the end of the year; the trial met with every success and increased the wages by about four and one-half per cent. In the Seventeenth Annual Report of the New Jersey Bureau of Statistics is the following remark: "It had a very salutary effect on the men, morally as well as economically, and upon the business success of the firm."

An important case of participation in the United States was that of Brewster & Co., New York, 1875. This firm carried on a plan of participation for two and one-half years. The firm manufactured carriages, and had about 450 employees. There had never been a strike or any other difficulty with labor. Mr. J. W. Britton was head of the firm and the chief sponsor of the plan.

Before adopting any definite plan, Mr. Britton made a serious study of the whole problem involved. He felt that under the different methods employed abroad there was one principal weakness, capital usually received its full share before labor received anything.

Britton conceived a very liberal plan; labor was given ten per cent of the gross profits before making any deductions for the salaries of the partners, or interest on capital. The money was to be distributed on the basis of the wages paid, and went to all workers who completed the fiscal year. An Industrial Association was formed to carry out the partnership idea. The workmen of each of the seven departments of the firm elected a board; the chairmen of these boards in turn formed a board of governors which elected a president (Mr. Britton) to head the whole association. This board regulated the internal affairs and relationship between employers and employed, made rules and regulations, and investigated complaints.

The employees had also the right to pass on pay increases passed by a majority of two-thirds of the employees. The president of the association could veto it, but if the employees passed it again, it became binding. Otherwise, the employees had no power over, or rights in the management of the firm, and the bonus was expressly declared to be a voluntary concession on the part of the company.

Some results: Although extensive powers were given to labor, they never took advantage of it in making unreasonable demands. The rules which the body of employees adopted were more severe than rules which the firm might otherwise have set for them. The quality of the product was improved thus giving a greater value to the products. Losses were greatly reduced, due to the greater care with which the work was done. For the first six months of 1870, the employees received a bonus of $5,000; for the second six months it amounted to $8,200. The bonus meant an increase of about three and one-half per cent in wages.

The firm of Charles A. Pillsbury & Co. was for some years the largest flour manufacturer and mill owner in the world. In 1874, the firm made possible the manufacturing of flour barrels by a cooperative organization, the Cooperative Barrel Mfg. Co., by purchasing their supply from that organization. In 1882, the management of the Pillsbury Flour Mills selected from among their group of from 400 to 500 employees about one-fourth, all of whom had served the company for five continuous years or more, and sent each an individual letter telling them that they had "decided to give this year as an experiment to some of the leading men in our different mills a portion of the net profits of the mills after we have credited ourselves with the interest on the capital invested.... This apportionment will be made only to the men who stay with us during the year, and is subject to the provision that every man included in the arrangement shall perform his work and conduct himself in a manner entirely satisfactory to us."[1] The distribution was made on the basis of salaries received and amounted to about one-third the yearly wages of the employees. During the following years the number of employees eligible for participation was increased so that by 1885 about one-third of all employees took part, a group which included all responsible employees in the office as well as in the mills. During 1885-1887 no

1. N. P. Gilman, Profit Sharing Between Employers and Employees, pp. 302-303.

bonuses were distributed because there were not enough profits, but another distribution was made in 1888. Before any distribution was made, the firm withdrew an amount equal to eight per cent interest on the capital from the yearly profit.

The advantage of the system was mainly to stabilize the working force. It also helped the firm to get better service from their employees.[1]

We may regard these attempts at participation and bonus payments as clear indications of the realization on the part of the owners or managers of business that something would have to be done in order to encourage the workers to increase output. In most of these schemes there was, however, a distinct lack of proper planning and investigation before they were put into practice; in fact, they were adopted for trial, and were very often dropped too early. The wide diversity of these plans is also indicative of the great individualism of the typical American businessman. The U. S. Commissioner of Labor points out in his first annual report, 1911, that labor should participate in the profits in proportion to their efficiency.[2]

But the attempts at basing these plans on knowledge gained by experience and scientific investigation and bringing into them some form of uniformity did not finally emanate from the businessman, who may either be the owner or manager of the firm, but it came from the man whose mind was scientifically trained, i.e., the engineer.

Pioneers of the Management Movement.

Just at the time when it was possible to remain entirely satisfied with things as they were, to consider profit-sharing as the "one" solution

1. Albert Shaw, Cooperation in a Western City, in Vol. 1, No. 4 of the publication of the American Economic Association, 188. Bemis, Part IV, V & VI on Cooperation in the Northwest, written by Dr. Albert Shaw, pp. 355-362.   N. P. Gilman, op. cit.,pp.301-305.
2. U. S. Commissioner of Labor, First Annual Report, 1911.

31

for our industrial ills, a group of men became active in emphasizing the
importance of management. This group of men were engineers, and at the
American Society of Mechanical Engineers[1] they held meetings and discussed
their problems.

Piece-work plans were far from perfect. The trouble was that
management did not know and had no means of determining the possible output by labor. In fact, some had come to believe that it was impossible
for management to determine it at all.

The papers[2] dealing with management read before the American
Society of Mechanical Engineers, were based on this impossibility. They
offered, therefore, a plan of compromise along the lines of profit-sharing.

The first paper, 1886, presented before the A. S. M. E. dealing
exclusively with the functions of management and stressing their importance
is that by Henry R. Towne of the Yale and Towne Manufacturing Company.
Towne's address was on "The Engineer as an Economist", and in many places,
it has been regarded as the beginning of the management movement.

According to Henry R. Towne, the final issue of the engineer's work
will resolve itself into a question of dollars and cents. This is
especially true in the case of the mechanical engineer since his functions,
more often than in the case of others, "include the executive duties of
organizing and superintending the operation of industrial establishments,
and of directing the labor of the artisans whose organized efforts yield
the fruition of his work.[3]

For the first time (1886) the importance of the mechanical engineer
is stressed in regard to his functions in management of the industrial

---

1. F. A. Halsey, The Premium Plan for Paying Labor, (Transactions of
American Society of Mechanical Engineers) Vol. 12, p. 759. 1890-1891.
2. Prof. W. Denton and H. R. Towne, Four Papers, (Transactions of American
Society of Mechanical Engineers) Vol. 10, p. 618. 1888-1889.
3. Henry R. Towne, The Engineer as an Economist, (Transactions of the
A. S. M. E.) Vol. 7, 1886, p. 428

enterprise. Towne goes further when he states what he regards as
essential for the successful management of an industrial enterprise:
"To insure the best results the organisation of productive labor must
be directed and controlled by persons having not only good executive
ability, but having an equally, practical knowledge of how to observe,
record, analyse, and compare essential facts in relation to wages,
supplies, expense accounts, and all else that enters into or affects the
economy of production and the cost of the product. There are many good
mechanical engineers; there are also many good 'businessmen'; but the
two are rarely combined in one person. But this combination of qualities,
together with at least some skill as an accountant, is essential to the
successful management of industrial works, and has its highest effectiveness if united in one person, who is thus qualified to supervise, either
personally or through assistants, the operations of all departments of a
business, and to subordinate each to the harmonious development of the
whole."[1]

This statement by Towne shows a full recognition of the problems
involved and the qualifications required for the successful management
of an industrial plant and had never been so fully brought out before.
He stresses the fact that shop management is of equal importance with
engineering since it affects the successful operation of almost all
industrial establishments, and for this reason "the management of works
has become a matter of such great and far-reaching importance as perhaps
to justify its classification as one of the modern arts."[2]

He regrets that each establishment starting de novo has to develop
its own system, without having the experience of others as a guide.

---

1. Henry R. Towne, op. cit., p. 428
2. Ibid., p. 429

The remedy cannot come from the businessmen alone, it has to come from those whose training and experience has given them an understanding of both the mechanical and clerical sides. For this reason Towne thinks that it should come from those who are engineers, especially mechanical engineers.

He then divides the work of the factory into two principal parts, i.e., Shop Management and Shop Accounting. A third head may be included in each of these, i.e., Shop Forms and Blanks. Under Shop management he includes questions pertaining to organization, responsibility, reports, systems of contracts and piece-work; under the questions on Shop Accounting come time and wage system, determination of cost, etc. Towne then stressed the function of forms and blanks as a means to expedite production and facilitate control.[1]

He also mentions an establishment, (although he does not mention it by name, we can readily surmise that it is the Towne and Yale Manufacturing Co.) which h a d a system of contract and piece-work for some fifteen years; as a result labor cost had been reduced considerably without encroaching upon the earnings of the men.

In the discussion which followed, W. E. Partridge gave an account of a piece-work system which he developed, but had not put in operation. This system provided for new piece-rates as soon as a man devised a plan or any new device by which the time required to perform a given operation could be shortened. The workmen received one-half of the gain made. If the improved method, machine, or tool originated in the drawing-room or office, the men got one-third and the establishment two-thirds of the savings. When the improved methods called for new tools, dies, jigs, etc.,

---

1. H. R. Towne, The Engineer as an Economist; A. S. M. E. Transactions, Vol. 7, 1886, pp. 427-432.

they were made at the expense of the firm at all times. This system helped to reduce the cost of production and increased wages at the same time.[1]

The next paper read before the Society at the same session in relation to management was that of William Kent of New York. It was entitled "A Problem in Profit-Sharing." Kent gave three hypothetical cases of manufacturing plants:

A. Introduces profit-sharing in the manufacturing plant through which the cost of production is decreased by one-fourth and the amount of production increased by 25 per cent.

B. Puts in new machinery, runs over-time, pays its workmen the same wages as before and doubles output.

C. Thinks that the selling cost is too high and for this reason cuts the cost in the sales department.

Results: A's cost of production (per unit) is five cents more than the selling price, hence it ends up with a loss.

B. doubles the profit and C. remains stationary, having neither an increase nor decrease in the amount of sales (number of units sold) while competition has been met through a proportional cut of expenses in the sales department.

The conclusion which Kent reached from these three hypothetical cases was that where the selling of the articles produced is entirely separate from the making of them, the share of the workmen should be calculated not on the profits of the whole business, but on the savings in the manufacturing department alone.[2]

---

1. H. R. Towne, op. cit., pp. 469-470.
2. William Kent, A Problem in Profit-sharing, A. S. M. E. Transactions, Vol. 8, 1887, pp. 630-633.

It is interesting to note the discussions which followed the reading of these papers. After the reading of the paper mentioned above, attention was drawn, by one gentleman who took part in the discussion, to the unprofitableness of over-time on account of (1) the higher pay required, (2) the fact that the work has to be done at night, which tends to reduce efficiency and output, (3) the worker, after having worked over-time is not able to accomplish so much the following day.

In the same discussion, H. R. Towne objected to the tendency of limiting the workman's share in the profits to the things which he can control, without taking cognizance of things he cannot control. He states: "The point is made that no profit-sharing is equitable unless it includes loss-sharing. Broadly stated, I think that perhaps this is true; but there are modifications in profit-sharing which eliminate this difficulty. The one which I ventured upon in a somewhat larger way after much study and consideration, may be more correctly designated as saving-sharing than as profit-sharing. It is based upon ascertaining the present cost of a given product in labor, or the things that labor can control, and then agreeing to divide any reduction which may be effected in the labor item below that cost with the producers; not giving them all of it by any means, possibly only one-half, but giving them some fraction which is equitable under all circumstances, and making an arrangement whereby these conditions will last for such a length of time as will give the producers an inducement to exert themselves to reduce the cost of production by earnest effort on their part."[1]

In the following year (1888) Towne read his paper on "Gain-Sharing" before the A. S. M. E. In it he explained more fully what he had already

1. William Kent, A Problem in Profit-Sharing, A. S. M. E. Transactions, Vol. 8, 1887, pp. 644-645.

alluded to in the discussion mentioned. He based the paper on Webster's
definition of profit as the excess of value over cost, and gain as meaning
that which is obtained at an advantage.

A manufacturer may concede some of the profits to the manufacturing
department of his establishment to be divided among labor, while another
part can be divided among his chief assistants. But the factors affecting
profits are becoming more and more complex, and, therefore, may be
divided into the following groups:

1. Those contributed by the owner or principal, such as capital,
   plant, character of building machinery; degree of ability, skill,
   experience, etc. of the owner himself--

2. Those influenced by the mercantile staff, buyer, etc.--

3. Those determined by causes beyond the control of the principal
   and his agents, such as fluctuations in cost of raw material, etc.--

4. Those influenced by his workmen or operatives, such as care of
   property, economy in the use of materials and supplies, and, chiefly,
   efficiency in the use of machinery and employment of labor.[1]

The following proposition is made to the employees:

"I have already ascertained the cost of our product in labor, supplies,
economy of material, and such other items as you can influence. I will
undertake and pay you for a system whereby the cost of product in these
same items will be periodically ascertained, and will agree to divide
among you a certain portion (retaining the remainder for myself) of any
gain, or reduction in cost which you may effect by reason of increased
efficiency of labor or increased economy in the use of material, or
both; this arrangement not to disturb your rates of wages, which are to
continue, as at present, those generally paid for similar services."[2]

---

1. H. R. Towne, Gain sharing, A. S. M. E. Transactions, Vol. 10,
   1888-1889, pp. 600-601.
2. Ibid., p. 603.

The system as proposed by Towne and which had already been in actual operation at the Yale and Towne Manufacturing Company for two years, provides for the conditions typified by the foregoing suppositious case. It aims at giving the employees a share in the gains or benefits accruing from their own efforts; it is thus not supposed to involve in the account the general profits and losses of the business. Towne thought that the system would work well in productive industries, especially in those whose product is of a simple or uniform kind, but could even be adapted so as to include large mercantile houses. The basis for such a system would be an accurate knowledge of the present cost of product (or, in the case of a mercantile establishment, the cost of operating it) which would have to be stated in terms so as to include the factors mentioned above and leaving out the factors on which labor in the manufacturing division has no influence; hence it must be based on the cost records. The data thus accumulated should stretch over a sufficiently long period. Towne suggests from six to twelve months so as to represent a fair mean or average.

In 1891, another paper was presented before the A. S. M. E. in an attempt at a solution of the wage problem. Frederick A. Halsey called his suggested system "The Premium Plan of Paying for Labor."

Before he presented his plan, Halsey criticized the different systems and methods under which labor was paid. His criticism[1] shows that management was aware of the shortcomings of the methods used in paying labor, and was endeavoring to find some satisfactory solution of the problem.

1. Under the Day's Work Plan the workman has no inducement at all to exert himself, and hence, does not exert himself.

2. Under the Piece Work Plan, the employer finds that work which costs

---

1. F. A. Halsey, Premium Plan for Paying Labor (Transactions of A. S. M. E.) Vol. 12, p. 759.

him one dollar could be done for 80¢, and as an inducement offers the workman 90¢, expecting that the output may be increased 25 per cent. Then the workman starts to astonish himself and all others by increasing his output far beyond the 25 per cent, but the cost of work remains where set, at ninety cents per piece.

In trying to lower the piece-rate, he may kill the goose that lays the golden eggs.

Under this plan, the employer has no benefit at all in any further saving of time.

2. Under the Profit-Sharing Plan the workmen are given a share in what they do not earn. Increased profits may arise from more systematic shop management, decreased expenses of the sales department, and many other causes with which the workman has nothing to do.

Further, the workmen share without individual desert. A workman, exerting himself because of the incentive, may have to divide the results of his efforts with less efficient men.

The author gives three additional scores against profit-sharing, the last one being that the system is an agreement between two parties, the first one having every temptation and opportunity to cheat the other, while the second has no means of knowing whether it has been cheated; this is because the workmen have no opportunity to examine the books and see for themselves whether the agreement is kept or not.[1]

With the Premium Plan Halsey tries to bring about a direct method of dividing the savings due to increased production. First, the time required to do a given piece of work is determined on the basis of previous experience. Then the workman is offered a premium for every

---

1. F. A. Halsey, The Premium Plan for Paying Labor; A. S. M. E. Transactions, Vol. 12, 1890-1891 (Canada) pp. 755-758.

hour by which he reduces the time set for the work, but this amount of premium is less than the hourly wage rate.

Halsey goes on to say: Making the hourly premium less than the hourly wages is the foundation stone on which rest all the merits of the system, since by it if an hour is saved on a given product the cost of the work is less and the earnings of the workman are greater than if the hour is not saved; the workman being in effect paid for saving time. In the extreme case, if the output he doubled, the wages paid per piece will be reduced 33⅓ per cent, but the workman's earnings per hour will be increased 33⅓ per cent. No cutting down of the rate should be made unless, indeed, improved processes destroy the significance of the first time base.[1]

In order to demonstrate more clearly the working of his plan, Halsey gave the following table:

Time Consumed Hours	Wages Per Piece	Premium	Total Cost of Work Col.2 + Col.3	Workman's Earnings Per Hour Col. 4 ÷ Col. 1
10	$3.00	$0	$3.00	$ .30
9	2.70	.10	2.80	.311
8	2.40	.20	2.60	.325
7	2.10	.30	2.40	.343
6	1.80	.40	2.20	.366
5	1.50	.50	2.00	.40

The case given here: Under the old plan a piece of work required ten hours for its production, and the wages paid are thirty cents per hour. The table shows the manner in which the cost diminishes and the workman's

---

1. F. A. Halsey, op. cit., pp. 759-60.

wages increase together.

The piece work plan does not apply to work of a jobbing nature; hence there can be no comparison between the two. The system is applicable to all kinds of machine work except jobbing, or work done by the hour.[1]

In the discussion which followed the reading of the paper, a remark was made to the effect that if such improvements could be made, then the employees, at day wages, had been robbing both the consumer and the employer. Kent testified also that they had already used the plan for three years without encountering any troubles in the plants of the Springer Torsion Balance Company. In criticism of the plan, we may note how small the increase in wages actually is compared with the increase in output. The worker is guaranteed his full day rate, and on what he produces above the minimum set he gets a premium of one-third of the day work cost. Its advantages are the simplicity with which rates are set since Halsey abandons any attempt at finding exact cost and uses as a basis simply past records. Another advantage is that the workman is assured of his day rate. To the employer the chief advantage is that it permits the pay of the worker to fluctuate only by one-third in relation to his output, thus minimizing the risk involved in making a mistake in setting the rate. And for the same reason, rates may also be regarded as more or less permanently set, and the workers need not thus restrict their output as they usually do under ordinary piece-work.

The Halsey system met with increasing favor and as early as 1902 was used in the U. S., Canada, England, Scotland, Germany, Italy, and Belgium. However, more serious attention was given to it in Great Britain than in any other country.

---

1. F. A. Halsey, op. cit., pp. 764.

Mention should be made of a system which is only a modification of the Halsey plan, and which has not met with great approval in the United States. It is known as the "Rowan Plan". The firm of David Rowan & Co. of Glasgow, makers of marine engines, was the first British firm (1902) to take an interest in the Halsey Plan. Halsey had in mind avoiding the cutting of rates. Rowan wanted to provide further against such a possibility, since, if output for instance, would increase tenfold, then wages may be so excessive as to force a cut. For this reason the plan provided that after a certain time had been allowed to the workman as standard time, wages should be increased by the same percentage as time for doing the work which is cut from the standard set. Thus, if the time is cut ten per cent, his wage rate per hour is increased by ten per cent. If be cuts the time twenty per cent, his wage-rate will be increased twenty per cent. But, when the wage has doubled the limit is reached, and no more increases are made. The increases in pay up to two-thirds of the economy are more liberal than under the Halsey Plan; from that time on further exertions on the part of the workman are not considered. The plan is one of extreme caution and shows a definite lack of confidence in the accuracy of the time set for a given job.

Taylor's Paper on a Piece Rate System.

The previous wage payment plans (1886 to 1895) all had the object of correcting the faults of the ordinary methods of paying labor. The Towne and Halsey plans had both served to draw attention to the labor situation and the problems connected therewith.

The new method of payment advocated by F. W. Taylor, 1895, which marks the inception of scientific management was a radical departure from all the previous systems and thus constitutes something new and unique compared with what had been done before in America and Europe.

According to Frederick Winslow Taylor's own remark, scientific management started in the fall of 1882. We can, therefore, roughly take the years from 1880 to 1890 as the period during which Taylor developed the principles of the science of management. In 1895, he read before the American Society of Mechanical Engineers a paper on "A Piece-Rate System, Being a Step Toward Partial Solution of the Labor Problem".[1]

The main object, according to Taylor, in the founding of scientific management was the solution of the wage problem. In the introduction to his paper, Taylor brings out the fact that piece-work "involves a permanent antagonism between employer and men, and a certainty of punishment for each man who reaches a high rate of efficiency. The demoralizing effect of this system is most serious. Under it, even the best workmen are forced continually to act the parts of hypocrites, to hold their own in their struggle against the encroachment of the employers."[2]

His own system, according to F. W. Taylor, however, works directly opposite, both in theory and practice. The employer's and employee's interests are the same, since under it a premium is paid for high efficiency. The worker will thus find that it is to his advantage to turn out the best quality as well as the maximum quantity of work.

The system itself, the principle of which "consists in paying men and not positions," is divided into these three elements:

1. An elementary rate fixing department.

2. The differential rate system of piece-work.

3. What he (Taylor) believes to be the best method of encouraging men who work by the day.

---

1. A. S. M. E. Transactions, Vol. 16, 1894-1895.
2. Ibid., p. 856.

Wages are fixed, as far as possible, according to the skill and energy with which man performs his work.

Among the risks of manufacturing, by far the most serious is that of bad management. Taylor then brings up the "soldiering" of labor; men work at the rate of one-third or even one-fourth of what they actually could do and the piece rates are based on such performance. Neither the "Gain-Sharing Plan" nor the "Premium Plan of Paying Labor" in any way remedies the situation, the former being slow and irregular in reducing cost, does not attract the first-class man, nor does it insure the maximum output per man and machine; and the latter still tempts labor to hold back and "soldier".

His own plan then is finally one of "Harmonizing of Conflicting Interests." The antagonism between employer and employed is because labor's universal aim is to receive the largest wages possible for their time, while the employer wants the largest possible return for the wages paid. According to Taylor, the basis for cooperation lies on the following two facts:

1. "That the workmen in nearly every trade can and will materially increase their present output per day, provided they are assured of a larger and permanent return for their time than they have heretofore received."

2. "That the employers can well afford to pay higher wages per piece even permanently, providing each man and machine in the establishment turns out a proportionately larger amount of work."[1]

---

1. F. W. Taylor, A Piece-Rate System, A. S. M. E. Transactions, Vol. 16, 1894-1895, p. 867.

These statements Taylor based on the fact that indirect expenses remain constant, whether the output is large or small.

In the solution of the piece-work problem, the most formidable obstacle is the lack of knowledge, on the part of both men and management, of the quickest time in which each piece of work can be done; or, briefly, the lack of accurate time-tables for the work of the place. The remedy for this trouble lies in the establishing in every factory of a proper rate fixing department; a department which shall have equal dignity and command equal respect with the engineering and managing departments, and which shall be organized and conducted in an equally scientific and practical manner.

Such a rate fixing department had been established at the Midvale Steel Company as early as 1883, at the time when he was working as a foreman of the machine shop. It had occurred to him that it was simpler to time each of the elements of the various kinds of work done in the place, and then find the quickest time in which each job could be done, by summing up the total times of its component parts, than it was to search through the records of former jobs, and guess at the proper price. After practicing this method of rate fixing himself for about a year, it became evident that the system was a success.

In connection with the establishment of these rates, in fact, before they could be definitely set, experiments were made on the work done by the metal cutting tools, such as lathes, planers, boring mills, etc. The laws governing the proper cutting speed of tools had to be determined first, formulated, and finally practically applied to each machine. The effect of the altering of the cutting speed of any of the following variables was studied: The shape of the tool (i.e., lip angle, clearance angle, and the line of the cutting edge), the duration of the cut, its depth, and the thickness of the feed or shaving.

Under an elementary system of rate-fixing an analysis of the following type would be made:

Work done by man	Minutes
Time to lift piece from floor to planer table	_ _ _ _
Time to level and set work true on table	_ _ _ _
Time to put on stops and bolts	_ _ _ _
Time to rough off cut ¼" thick, 4' long, etc.	_ _ _ _
Time to rough off cut 1/8" thick, 3' long, 12" wide	_ _ _ _
Time to finish cut 4' long, 2½" wide, etc.	_ _ _ _ [1]

Thus the fundamental principle is to divide a task into its simple elements.

Once we have made a study of the time required to do a certain kind of work, the next problem, according to Taylor, is to get the best men who will work at the fastest speed, or anywhere near it, in order to obtain a maximum output in the shop. The most effective means to find such men has proved to be the differential rate system of piece-work. This consists, briefly, in paying a higher price per piece, or per unit, or per job, if the work is done in the shortest possible time, and without imperfections, than is paid if the work takes a longer time or is imperfectly done.

To illustrate: Suppose 20 units .to be the largest amount of work of a certain kind that can be done in a day. Under the differential rate system, if a workman finishes 20 pieces per day, and all of these pieces are perfect, he receives, say 15¢ per piece, making his pay for the day .15 x 20 = $3. If, however, he works too slowly, and turns out, say, only 19 pieces, then instead of receiving 15¢ per piece, he gets only 12¢ per piece, making his pay for the day .12 x 19 = $2.28,....

_____

1. F. W. Taylor, op. cit., p. 871.

If he succeeds in finishing 20 pieces, some of which are imperfect, then he should receive a still lower rate of pay, say 10¢ or 5¢ per piece, according to the circumstances.[1]

In order to understand this method of payment, management must recognize some fundamental principles and·facts. The most important of these facts is that men will not do an extraordinary day's work for an ordinary day's pay. Justice, however, not only demands for the workman an increased reward for a large day's work, but should compel him to suffer an appropriate loss in case his work falls off either in quantity or quality.

The lower differential rate should be fixed at a figure which will allow the workman to earn scarcely an ordinary day's pay when he falls off from his maximum pace, so as to give him every inducement to work hard and well.

It is not, however, sufficient that each workman's ambition should be aroused by the prospect of larger pay at the end of even a short (comparatively) period of time. The stimulus to maximum exertion should be a daily one.

This method can also be applied where the work is done by gangs. There, the differential rate acts as the most powerful lever to force each man in a gang of workmen to do his best; because, through the carelessness or laziness of any one man, the gang fails to earn its high rate, the drone will surely be obliged by his companions to do his best the next time or else get out.

Taylor sees in this method the greatest advantage in that it

---

1.   F. W. Taylor, op. cit., pp. 871-872.

produces the right mental attitude on the part of both management and
men. Under the differential rate system, it is their common interest
to cooperate to the fullest extent and to devote every energy to turning
out daily the largest possible output. This common interest quickly
replaces antagonism and establishes a most friendly feeling.

A careful study of the capabilities of the machines, and the
analysis of the speed at which they must run, before differential rates
can be fixed which will insure their maximum output, almost invariably
results in first indicating and then correcting the defects of their
design and in the method of running and caring for them.

Output of both machine and man must be materially increased, hence
the proper man must be found for each job and the proper incentives be
offered to him in order to make the system successful.

Since the cost of operating a machine will be the same regardless
of the number of pieces produced, Taylor gives the following table with
which he demonstrates the effectiveness of his system:

Cost of Production per Lathe per Day

Ordinary System of Piece-Work		Differential Rate System	
Man's Wages	2.50	Man's Wages	3.50
Machine Cost	3.37	Machine Cost	3.37
Total Cost per Day	$5.87	Total Cost per Day	$6.87
5 pieces produced		10 pieces produced	
Cost per piece	$1.17	Cost per piece	$0.69[1]

In the discussion which followed the reading of this paper, William
Kent said that while he was using the Halsey Plan, he felt that in his

---

1. F. W. Taylor, op. cit., p. 879.

opinion Taylor's plan was a little ahead. Taylor also mentioned that his plan had been in successful operation for the past ten years, (1885-1895) but from Halsey's criticism we can safely assume that it had not become general knowledge before the paper was read at the A. S. M. E.

Taylor claimed the following advantages for his system:

1. That the manufacturers are producing more cheaply under it, while at the same time the workmen earn higher wages than are usually paid.

2. Since the rate fixing is done from accurate knowledge instead of more or less by guesswork, the motive for holding back on work, or "soldiering", and endeavoring to deceive the employer as to the time required to do work, is entirely removed and with it the greatest cause for hard feelings and war between the management and the men.

3. Since the basis from which piece work as well as day rates is fixed by exact observation, instead of being founded upon accident or deception, as it..., the men are treated with greater uniformity and justice, and respond by doing more and better work.

4. It is for the common interest of both the management and the men to cooperate in every way....

5. The system is rapid, while other systems are slow, in attaining the maximum productivity of each machine and man; and when this maximum is once reached, it is automatically maintained by the differential rate.

6. It automatically selects and attracts the best men for each

---

1. F. W. Taylor, op. cit., p. 884 and p. 886.

class of work, and it develops many first-class men who would otherwise remain slow or inaccurate while at the same time it discourages
and sifts out men who are incurably lazy or inferior.

7. One of the chief advantages...that it promotes most friendly feelings
between the men and their employers, and so renders labor unions and
strikes unnecessary.[1]

Introduction of Taylor's Ideas in the Shop.

The application of Taylor's system meant such a departure from past
method and practice and in the following years caused so much public attention and disputes that it seems to warrant a closer study of the man
as well as the firms in which his methods were first developed.

At the age of 22 Taylor went as a day laborer to the Midvale Steel
Works which had been established in 1867, shortly after the close of the
Civil War. This was about the time when the open-hearth process was
perfected commercially.

In 1873, Sellers had become president of the company. In referring
to Sellers, Taylor spoke of him as "undoubtedly the most noted engineer
in this country in his time, a truly scientific experimenter and a bold
innovator", and "a man way beyond his generation of progress."[2]

Sellers believed that when a machine was right, it would look right.
He insisted on weeding out non-essentials; everything about a machine
should be directly contributory to the purpose for which the machine was
made.

There were three able men at the steel works, Charles A. Brinley,
who in 1872 entered as a chemist; Russell W. Davenport, also a scientifically

1. F. W. Taylor, op. cit., pp. 657-858.
2. Frank Barkley Copley, Frederick W. Taylor, Father of Scientific Management," Vol. I, p. 108.

trained man, and Ouilliaem Aertsen, who was an able assistant to the
other two. These three men were in charge of operations when Taylor
entered the employ of the company.[1]

The best description of how Taylor developed and applied his
original ideas on management is obtained from his direct testimony
before the Special Committee of Congress years later:

"In 1878, I came to the Midvale Steel Works as a day laborer, after
having served two apprenticeships as a pattern maker and a machinist.
I came there as a laborer because I could not get work at my trade.
Work at that time was very dull — it was toward the end of the long
period of depression following the panic of 1873. I was assigned to
work on the floor of the machine shop. Soon after I went there, the
clerk of the shop got mixed up in his accounts, and they thought he was
stealing — I never could quite believe that he was; I thought it was
merely a mix up — and they put me in to take his place, simply because I was able to do clerical work."

"I did this clerical work all right, although it was distasteful
to me, and after having trained another clerk in to do the work of the
shop, I asked permission of the foreman to work as a machinist. They
gave me a job on the lathe because I had made good as a clerk when they
needed me, and I worked for some time with the lathe gang.

"Shortly after this, they wanted a gang boss to take charge of the
lathes, and they appointed me to this position."[2]

However, we are more interested in what Taylor did at Midvale and
how scientific management was introduced there. From his own testimony

1. F. B. Copley, op. cit., pp. 111-112.
2. Eastern Rate Case Hearings, p. 1411. (Vol. 3)

we see that in a short period he became gang boss. According to his
own words, he knew that workmen were "soldiering" from the time of his
apprenticeship. "I absolutely knew it. I saw the same thing, Mr.
Chairman, all through my apprenticeship; from the time I started as an
apprentice until I got through the thing was practically universal in
the shop."[1]

But while a laborer, he had played fair; he knew the reason for
it. Workers were afraid the piece-rates would be cut; they feared and
believed there was just so much work to be done and not more, and setting
a quicker pace would result in a lowering of wages and unemployment. "We
who were the workmen of that shop had the quantity output carefully
agreed upon for everything that was turned out in the shop. We limited
the output to about, I should think, one-third of what we could very
well have done. We felt justified in doing this, owing to the piece-
work system, that is, owing to the necessity for soldiering under the
piece-work system."[2]

Once Taylor was promoted to gang boss, his attitude changed; he
was now on the side of management. According to Brinley, management had
already begun to manifest aloofness from the workmen, and he had set
piece-rates high enough to be regarded a proper incentive to put in a
fair day's work. The rest was left to the workman.

Taylor had no definite plans as to how he was going to accomplish
his new job as gang boss. Thinking the matter over, however, he realized
that the one thing which management lacked more than anything else was
exact knowledge as to how long it should take a workman to do his work.

1. Eastern Rate Case Hearings, p. 1428. (Vol. 8)
2. Ibid., p. 1411.

So he went to Sellers, and asked the permission to make a series of careful experiments to find out how quickly the various kinds of work that came into the shop ought to be done. He did more than this; he asked the full backing from Sellers for any change which he might institute. In 1884, Taylor was promoted to Chief Engineer of the plant by Davenport, who was then superintendent, but it was not until 1887, when Harrah had bought control of the company that he was formally elected to that position by the directors.

As soon as Taylor became gang boss, the men who were working under him knew that he was on to the whole game of soldiering or deliberately restricting output. So they came to him at once and said, "Now Fred, you are not going to be a piece-work hog, are you?"

"If you fellows mean you are afraid I am going to try to get a larger output from these lathes," I said, "Yes, I do propose to get more work out. You must remember I have been square with you fellows up to now and worked with you. I have not broken a single rate; I have been on your side of the fence. But now I have accepted a job under the management of this company, and I am on the other side of the fence, and I will tell you perfectly frankly, that I am going to try to get a bigger output from those lathes." "We fought on the management's side with all of the usual methods, and the workmen fought on their side with all of their usual methods."

Taylor was primarily a trained engineer; he was enthusiastic about what he was trying to do and in spite of his exacting nature, the workmen really admired him. As Copley says, after having talked to several workmen at the Midvale Steel Works: "he found that in every case they expressed for Fred Taylor admiration and affection running on into reverence and worship."[1] Even in those early days, the trained engineer

---

1. F. B. Copley, op. cit., p. 172.

was considered the best type of factory manager.

Mr. Otterson (J. E. Otterson, Pres. Winchester Repeating Arms Co.) wrote as follows: "The engineering type of man works for the solution of a single technical or engineering problem and is concerned with the determination of the solution rather than the application of that solution to practical activities. The true type has the capacity to concentrate continuously on a single problem until the solution has been reached. He is interested in the determination of cause and effect and of the laws that govern phenomena. He is disposed to be logical, analytical, studious, synthetical and to have an investigating turn of mind. The predominating characteristic that distinguishes him from the executive is his ability to concentrate on one problem to the exclusion of others for a protracted period, to become absorbed in that problem and free his mind of the cares of other problems. He does not submit readily to the routine performance of a given quantity of work. He deals with laws and abstract facts. . . Mr. Taylor was in reality an engineer rather than an executive. He applied his wonderful inventive genius to the invention of management methods."[1]

It can readily be seen how closely this characterization agrees with the facts. When Taylor was put in charge of the men, he had not yet clearly in mind what measures he would be going to take, no clear policy. He hoped the men could be persuaded to do more work, but he soon found out that this was out of the question. Hence, he first concentrated on breaking up "soldiering." The second step was to find the quickest time by which he meant "the quickest proper time" in which

1. Annals of the American Academy of Political and Social Science, Vol. 85, September 1919, p. 91. Quoted also in F. B. Copley, Vol. 1, pp. 148-149.

the work could be done by the workmen under such conditions that he would not meet with the slightest interruption or delay. He checked, for instance, the time it would take a workman to turn an axle and would then make an allowance for unavoidable accidents and delays. In doing this he would say to the workman, "I want you to cooperate with me in arriving at the truth regarding this fact." He then made the tests frequently for several days until he was able to agree with the workmen on what was the proper time. The next step was to get a "first-class man" to do the job.

"What I want to make clear is that each type of man is 'first-class' at some kind of work, and if you hunt far enough, you will find some kind of work that is especially suited to him."[1]

Another point or principle involved is that of standardization and control. Under Taylor's new system, studies would be made in motions, and these would then be standardized. To do a given job in the shortest possible time, it was essential to leave out unnecessary motions in order to save time as well as strength. And once a standard was set for a given task, the workman was instructed in these standards, was told and shown what the proper motions to do the job were, and it was only after he had learned all this, that he was expected to come up to the standard of output set for him.

Taylor pointed out time and again that scientific management involves a complete mental revolution on the part of the workingmen as well as on the part of the management. On the part of the men the attitude toward their duties, their work and their fellow-men has to change. The

---

1. Eastern Rate Case Hearings, Vol. 3, p. 1455.

management has to take a different attitude, from the foreman up to
the superintendent and finally the owner of the business, including
the board of directors. Without this mental change, scientific management does not exist.

"It is along this line of complete change in the mental attitude
of both sides; of the substitution of peace for war; the substitution
of hearty, brotherly cooperation for contention and strife; both pulling
hard in the same direction instead of pulling apart; of replacing
suspicious watchfulness with mutual confidence; of becoming friends instead of enemies, it is along this line, I say, that scientific management must be developed...."[1]

Much objection has been made to the use of the word "science" in
connection with scientific management. "I am much amused," says Taylor,
"to find that this objection comes chiefly from the professors of this
country. They resent the use of the word science for anything quite
so trivial as the ordinary, every-day affairs of life." As an answer
to such criticism, Taylor gives a definition of science as given by
President McLaurin of the Institute of Technology of Boston, who defined the word science as "classified or organized knowledge of any
kind."[2]

In his defense of scientific management, Taylor compared it with
the management of a first-class American baseball team. In a team
almost all the elements of scientific management are found, since every
element of the game of baseball has been subject to the most intimate

---

1. Eastern Rate Case Hearings, p. 13891
2. Ibid., p. 1394.

and close study of many men, and the best way of doing each act has been
agreed upon. From this, standards have been set which are accepted
throughout the country.

Taylor's methods and work at Midvale brought about a great and
fundamental change in management, in fact he developed an entirely new
type of organization. Until 1880, a foreman had supreme command and
discharged his duties personally or through his subordinates, but the
orders came from the former. Taylor employed a man to make time studies.
Once this man had accumulated enough data he started to write out instruction cards in which the workmen were told in detail what to do,
and the time it should take them. This, however, developed into a new
and separate function, namely that of seeing what work had to be done
and was being done by the men as recorded on their tickets; this brought
about the formation of a planning department. In this way, two main
functions were detached from the foreman, i.e., time study and planning.

One of the men was called the time clerk, and the other the instruction clerk. The cards which the latter made and which were based
on actual investigation, did not first pass through the hands of the
foreman, but they went to the worker directly. This was entirely opposed
to the old order, which Taylor called the military type and in which an
order was passed to the subordinate through his immediate superior.
Under the new method the foremen and gang bosses who were in direct
charge of the men were now restricted in their functions to executing
orders.

This was an entirely new organization; to put it in Taylor's own
words, "Thus we have a radically new, and what at first appears exceedingly confusing state of things, in which every man, foreman as well as

workman, receives and obeys orders f r o m o t h e r men, and in the case
of the various functional foremen, they continually give orders in their
own particular line to the very men from whom they are receiving orders
in other lines. For this reason the work of the Planning Department
represents an intricate mass of interwoven orders or directions, proceed-
ing between the men in charge of the various functions of management."[1]

Gradually, the functions of the old time foreman were further split
by Taylor into those of the gang boss, speed boss, inspector and repair
boss. When he started with his fining system, another man had to be
added, i.e., the shop disciplinarian who was in charge of the hiring, and
whose duties were identical with those of the modern employment or personnel
manager. This meant a breaking down of the task into its principal
functions of planning, preparation, scheduling, production and inspection
as we have it today, and according to which the three first functions are
regarded as those rightfully belonging under the domain of the engineer,
while production and inspection are regarded as executive functions.

While in his "Piece Rate System" Taylor does not mention functional
management, Taylor writes, however, in his "Shop Management": "The writer
introduced five of the elements of functional foremanship into the management of the small machine shop of the Midvale Company of Philadelphia
while he was foreman of that shop in 1882-1885; (1) the instruction card
clerk, (2) the time clerk, (3) the inspector, (4) the gang boss, and
(5) the shop disciplinarian. Each of these functional foremen dealt
directly with the workmen instead of giving their orders through the
gang boss.

---

1. From a manuscript prepared for his Harvard Lectures as reproduced
   in Copley, Vol. 1, p. 290.

"The dealings of the instruction card clerk and time clerk with the workmen were mostly in writing, and the writer himself performed the functions of shop disciplinarian, so that it was not until he introduced the inspector, with orders to go straight to the men, instead of the gang boss, that he appreciated the desirability of functional foremanship as a distinct principle in management. The prepossession in favor of the military type was so strong with the managers and owners of Midvale that it was not until years after functional foremanship was in continual use in this shop that he dared to advocate it to his superior officers as the correct principle."[1]

But while Taylor retained the name "boss" these functional foremen were to be considered more as teachers and friends. They were to study the work in advance and act as guides to the worker. The planning department was to analyse and study every job in advance, give written orders and to instruct each worker in: "the most minute detail of each motion which he is to make and the time in which he is to do it." All the implements the workman uses are not only specified, but systematically brought to him before he starts work.

With respect to the functions of the bosses, he says: "As the workman proceeds with a job, several teachers, one after another, come to him at his machine, and show him just how each motion is to be made in the most effective way. One of these teachers (called the inspector) sees to it that he understands the drawings and instructions for doing the work.

"He teaches him how to do work of the right quality, and how to make it fine and exact where it should be fine, and rough and quick

1. F. W. Taylor, <u>Shop Management</u>, New York 1911, p. 107.

where accuracy is not required, ---- the one being just as important for success as the other. The second teacher (the gang boss) shows him how to set up the job in his machine, and teaches him how to make all his personal motions in the quickest and best way. The third (the speed boss) sees that the machine is run at the best speed, and that the proper tool is used in the particular way which will enable the machine to finish its product in the shortest possible time. In addition to the assistance given by these teachers, the workman receives orders and help from four other men; from the repair boss as to adjustment, cleanliness and general care of his machine, belting, etc.; from the time clerk, as to everything relating to his pay and to proper written reports and returns; from the route clerk, as to the order in which he does his work and as to the movement of the work from one part of the shop to another; and finally, in case a workman gets into trouble with any of his various bosses, the disciplinarian interviews him."[1]

For three years prior to 1890, the Midvale Steel Company worked on orders for the army and navy, and it was through this contact that Taylor became known to men high in the government service. Among others, he came in contact with William C. Whitney, then Secretary of the Navy Department. In 1889, Whitney became interested in the Manufacturing Investment Company which was being organized in New York to exploit a patented process to convert wood products into fibre for the manufacturing of paper. When the stage was set, Taylor received a definite offer to become manager. He left Midvale and accepted the offer under a three year contract. This new venture did not prove to be successful financially, but it showed Taylor the need for consulting engineers in management.

---

1. From a manuscript prepared by Taylor for his Harvard Lectures in 1909, as quoted in Copley, Vol. 1, pp. 324-325.

What induced him to become a consulting engineer in management was the fact that he had felt the double duty of being manager of an establishment and systematising and introducing his system at the same time was too much of a task; and he considered a separation of these duties desirable. During this time he had prepared a rubber stamp reading as follows:

> FRED W. TAYLOR, M. E.,
>
> Ross Street, Germantown, Philadelphia.
>
> Consulting Engineer
>
> Systematising Shop Management And
>
> Manufacturing Costs A Specialty

This meant that he did not offer his services as a manager, but for the special purpose of systematising and organising the work. While working for the Manufacturing Investment Company, he had come in contact with the professional accountant Basley, whom he now summoned to his assistance, and with him, he went through all the problems of accounting and systems of cost accounting. In the same year, he read his "Notes on Belting" before the A. S. M. E. This was his first paper (1895) and public utterance. It was completely devoted to the subject of belting, but it gave a clear conception of his scientific approach.

At the Simonds Rolling Machine Company, Taylor's first client, he was involved in accounting work. It was here that the mnemonic classification of accounts was first put to practical use. He also used a work or distribution sheet for the proper distribution of overhead cost between the departments. It was here that he worked out the first purchase requisition with up-to-date store tag numbers and "material issued" and "material delivered" slips. A new feature which he introduced into accounting at this time was the "machine dollar hour", a record which drew attention to the cost of maintaining idle machinery.

In 1894, Taylor worked at the Cramp's Shipyards in Philadelphia. A preliminary report shows he proposed to set up standard conditions in regard to (1) belting, (2) automatic tool grinding, (3) tool rooms, storerooms, and tool making, and (4) the speeding of the machines. Here he was dealing with the shop only, and not with the cost system. It was here, however, that he continued working on his investigation into the art of cutting metals to "determine the relative cutting speeds of the Mushet and the carbon tool," the result of which eventually led to the discovery of "high-speed steel."

The following year (1896) he worked at the Steel Motor Works. Here he devised a complete classification of accounts with mnemonic symbols which are in use today. This meant that the first letters of the alphabet were used for the overhead expense accounts, the middle letters for the product accounts, and the last letters for the asset accounts.

During the period from 1897 to 1898 Taylor was employed at the Simonds Company, which manufactured bicycle balls. Since the factory had been shut down and moved to another building when Taylor came, he concentrated his attention on increasing the output, so as to enable the company to meet the accumulated demand. In order to do this, Taylor began by placing the men in the slowest, and then the next slowest departments on piecework. Up to that time they had received day wages. The result of the change was that with the same number of men and machines, production was increased from an average of 5,000,000 to 17,000,000 balls per month.

After having analysed the twenty or more operations involved in manufacturing bicycle balls, he came to the conclusion that the most important of all was the final inspection. This work was being done by girls who were working ten and one-half hours a day. As Taylor writes, "A most casual study made it evident that a very considerable part of the ten and one-half hours during which the girls were supposed to work was really spent in idleness because the working period was too long."[1] Hence, he went ahead and cut the hours first to ten, then to nine and one-half, then to nine and finally to eight and one-half hours. At each reduction in hours worked, production increased. He then employed Sanford E. Thompson who, under the superintendence of Gantt, made time and motion studies on the whole group.

The final result was "that thirty-five girls did the work formerly done by one hundred and twenty. And the accuracy of the work at the higher speed was two-thirds greater than before."[2]

Taylor mentions, however, "that the one element which did more than all the others was, the careful selection of girls with quick perception to replace those whose perception was slow."[3]

In 1898, Taylor had had a call from his old boss from Midvale, Russell W. Davenport, who was now second Vice-president of the Bethlehem Iron Company. As a result, he went to work in May of 1898.

In 1899, he brought in Carl G. Barth, a mathematical genius who had

1. F. W. Taylor, Principles of Scientific Management; The Plimpton Press, Norwood, Massachusetts; p. 87.
2. Ibid., p. 95.
3. Ibid., pp. 96-97.
    For full account on the work at the Simonds Co., see: Ibid., pp. 87-97; Copley, vol. 1, pp. 458-465; Drury, Horace, Bookwater, Scientific Management, A History and Criticism; New York, Columbia Univ. 1915 (Studies in History, Economics and Public Law) p. 102.

been for fourteen years with the William Sellers Company. At the time
he left there he was chief designer; when Taylor heard of him, he was
teaching mathematics and manual training at the Ethical Culture School
in New York.

Taylor had given much time and thought to the problem of getting
a quick solution for the proper feed and speed in the cutting of metals;
while Sinclair had worked out the formulae in 1883, the question of
getting quick answers to meet every-day requirements in the machine shop
had remained unanswered. Taylor had put several young college men to
work on the problem, and when Barth came a "Gantt-Knox instrument" was
already in use; this was an especially made slide rule accompanied by
diagrams, by means of which a more rapid solution to the speed and feed
problem was obtained.

Barth studied the problem by first making an "independent study" of
the Mannheim slide rule and the Sexton omnimeter which were then extensively used. First, he made a logarithmic slide rule in circular
form which was patterned after the Sexton instrument. This was not
quite satisfactory. He next designed a straight slide rule on which
the "scales were so constructed and arranged relatively to each other
that the proper feed and speed combination was at once revealed to the
eye," and it marked a full and direct solution towards which Taylor
had been aiming. How greatly Taylor valued this invention is best
expressed in his own words:

"The gain from these slide rules is far greater than that of all
the other improvements combined because it accomplishes the original
object for which in 1880 the experiments were started; i.e., that of
taking the control of the machine shop out of the hands of the many
workmen, and placing it completely in the hands of the management,

thus superseding 'rule of thumb' by scientific control."[1]

Taylor was employed to systematize the work done in the company's shop, and to introduce piece work. He started with the yard labor where from four to six hundred men were employed unloading railway cars and shoveling on to piles, and from these piles loading again as required.

The work covered a large variety of labor. Up to the Spring of 1899, this work had been done by gangs of men working by the day, and the men received $1.15 per day." From among these men, Taylor selected the pig iron handlers. This was the lowest and cheapest form of labor. The only tool a man needed in order to do this work were wide leather straps with which to protect his hands.

The first step taken was to break down the work into its elements. This was simple for this kind of work. In the case of a man loading pig iron on a car, the following would be the elements:
"(a) picking up the pig from the ground or pile (time in hundredths of a minute); (b) walking with it on a level (time per foot walked); (c) walking with it up an incline to car (time per foot walked); (d) throwing the pig down (time in hundredths of a minute), or laying it on a pile (time in hundredths of a minute); (e) walking back empty to get a load (time per foot walked)."[2]

Once this study was made, a task was set which was from three and one-half to four times as much work as the past average had been. But

---

1. F. W. Taylor, <u>On The Art of Cutting Metals</u>; The American Society of Mechanical Engineers, New York 1906; pp. 11-12.
2. F. W. Taylor, <u>Shop Management</u>, pp. 47-48.

before this could be done, he had to know how much a man could do without being overworked. He set Barth the task of solving this problem.
The pigs to be handled weighed 92 pounds each, and it was finally found
that a man could only be 43 per cent of the day under this load, while
57 per cent of the day he must be entirely free. As the weight becomes
lighter, the percentages of the day under which the man can remain under
the load increases. So that, if the workman is handling a half-pig,
weighing 46 pounds, he can be under the load 58 per cent of the day,
and only has to rest during 42 per cent.[1] Once this was ascertained,
Taylor started the now famous "Schmidt" on his task of handling forty-
seven tons of pig iron a day. Of him Taylor says:

"He regarded his task as an entirely fair one, and earned on an
average from the start $1.85 per day, which was sixty per cent more
than he had been paid by the day. This man happened to be considerably
lighter than the average workman at this class of work. He weighed
about 130 pounds; he proved, however, to be especially well suited to
this job, and was kept at it steadily throughout the time that the
writer was in Bethlehem, and some years later was still at the same
work."[2]

When Taylor wanted to start off the other men on the same basis
(i.e., on piece-work), he not only found them unwilling, but met with
opposition from some men of the management and from leading citizens
of Bethlehem. "One after another of the new men who were started
singly on this job were either persuaded or intimidated into giving
it up. In many cases they were given other work, at wages higher

---

1. F. W. Taylor, Principles of Scientific Management, pp. 56-58.
2. F. W. Taylor, Shop Management, p. 60.

than the ruling wages."[1] While opposition in the yard finally subsided since many of the laborers could not stand seeing one of their fellow workers making $1.85 while they received $1.15, Taylor and his staff found, however, that only one man out of eight was able to do the task.

From such studies standards were set. A standard was to Taylor "a criterion or model established as a result of scientific investigation," as opposed to the then prevailing definition of a standard as being "a criterion established by custom, public opinion, or general consent."[2] The setting of standards in the shop also brought changes about in the cost and accounting system. Taylor regarded the method of bookkeeping as practiced under the modern railroad system of accounting, when adapted to suit the manufacturing business, as the best available.

Another important event which took place while Taylor was at Bethlehem was the development of metal cutting.

According to Copley, it was just eight days after Maunsel White joined Taylor in the investigation on what tools to use, that the discovery was made which led to "high-speed Steel",[3] and from which the Taylor-White Process of heating tools developed. This discovery was that tools made from chromium-tungsten steels when heated to the melting point would do from two to four times as much work as other tools, or in Taylor's own words:

"Heating chromium-tungsten tools close to the melting point does not give them a degree of hardness which is unusual in tools, but it does give them the entirely new and extraordinary property of retaining

---

1. F. W. Taylor, Shop Management, pp. 50-51.
2. F. B. Copley, Vol. I., p. 346.
3. Ibid., Vol. 2, p. 79.

what hardness they have, even after the tool has been heated through
the pressure and friction of the chip, until it is almost red hot.
This new property in high speed tools has been very appropriately
named 'RED HARDNESS', because the tool maintains its cutting edge
sufficiently sharp and hard to cut steel even after its nose is red
hot, and because in many cases it heats up the chip or shaving which
it is cutting until the portions of the chip which are exposed to the
friction of the tool become red hot.... As to our invention, briefly
speaking, by far the most important of the several discoveries made
by us, and which led to the modern high speed tools, was the discovery
that when tools made from tool steel in its usual chemical composition
(containing not less than one-half of one per cent of chromium and not
less than one per cent of tungsten, or its equivalent) was treated in
a new and completely revolutionary manner to an extraordinarily high
heat, this treatment imparted an entirely new quality or property to
a cutting tool, namely the property called "red hardness"; and it is
this new property which enables these tools to run at their high cutting
speeds."[1]

Thus it is the quality of "red hardness" which was the essence of
the discovery. These chromium-tungsten tools would be ruined when
heated between 1,500 to 1,725 degrees Fahrenheit, but when they were
subjected to greater heat, the cutting efficiency would increase progressively, the greatest improvement taking place just before the melting
point, or at the maximum temperature to which the tool could be subjected without being destroyed.

Says Taylor: "These experiments corroborated our Cramp-Sellers
experiments, showing that the tools were seriously broken down or injured by

---

1. F. B. Copley, op. cit., pp. 192-193.

overheating, say, somewhere between 1550 degrees F. and 1700 degrees F.;
but to our great surprise, tools heated up to or above the high heat of
1725 degrees F. proved better than any of those heated to the best
previous temperature, namely, a bright cherry red; and from 1725° F. up
to the incipient point of fusion of the tools, the higher the temperature
the higher the cutting speeds at which they would run."[1]

Through further experimenting, Taylor and White perfected their
process of hardening tool steel and obtained two patents on it, which
they sold in 1900 to the Bethlehem Steel Company.

This new process doubled the capacity of every machine shop in the
world, as well as the efficiency of the workers employed; and cut in
half the capital needed to produce the same volume of work that was
necessary before the discovery was made.[2]

Lyndall Urick, in his   report distributed to members of the
                                        in 1938
Seventh International Management Congress in London/said in relation
to the importance of this discovery:

"At the turn of the century activity in the management field in
Great Britain died down -- not because her managers were conservative
but because her established supremacy in the steel and machine tool
trades was seriously challenged by Taylor's invention of high speed
steel. Her engineering industry devoted itself almost exclusively for
rather more than a decade to the technical problems presented by that

1. F. B. Copley, op. cit., p. 24.
2. The best account of the whole discovery is given in Taylor's own
    lecture "On The Art of Cutting Metals"; an address given at
    the opening of the annual meeting of the A. S. M. E. in
    New York, December 1906. The history of his experiments is
    given on pp. 9 to 11; a full account is also given in Copley,
    Frederick W. Taylor, Father of Scientific Management, Vol. 2,
    pp. 79-118.

discovery. ——— It is in line with the irony which sometimes illumines human affairs that Taylor's own invention should have been the chief agency in distracting British attention from his still more important work in the management field."[1]

Significant Results of this Period of Flux

The sporadic, unrelated, and sometimes opposing activities that characterise this period were all looking toward the development and expression of better methods and practices, particularly in the field of shop management. The nature of the relationships between the various industrial sections of the country and the rapidity with which manufacturing enterprises were developing and new enterprises being started, together with the lack of adequate communication facilities, made the problem of interchange of ideas and experiences somewhat difficult. The recognition of the need for such informal and formal discussions of mutual problems and practices brought about the formation of the American Society of Mechanical Engineers in 1885. At its inception, the purpose of the Society was primarily to exchange information among the members relating to technical engineering subject matter and to serve as a vehicle for the development and exploration of the ideas and practices suggested in such papers as those presented by Frederick W. Taylor, Major Metcalf, and others. These papers dealt primarily with techniques and practices in shop management and expressed also some of what we now consider the fundamentals of good labor relations. The attitude of labor was not receptive with respect to the practices suggested by these writers, and in order to unify the labor front need and later to give labor a stronger voice in matters affecting its own welfare, we find a number of more or

1. L. Urick, The Development of Scientific Management in Great Britain. (British Management Review, Vol. 3, No. 4, p. 10)

less ineffective and weak labor organisations combining to form the American Federation of Labor. Their efforts were not productive in the new organisation until the turn of the century although the mere act of its formation brought sharply to the attention of business leaders the fact that labor would be sooner or later a far more important factor in the management of business and would need to be dealt with in a manner that would hereafter satisfy both the workers and the employers. Perhaps this recognition had much to do with the ready acceptance of some of the ideas relating to incentive wages, fatigue, and definite standards of problems suggested by Taylor and others in their early papers during the early life of the A. S. M. E. Although these developments were significant, they concentrated attention largely upon shop practices and the problems of operations in the shop rather than the broader field of scientific management. The widespread growth of interest in this later subject did not manifest itself until later in the twentieth century. The high lights of its development during this period will be found at the beginning of Chapter 5.

CHAPTER IV

CRYSTALLIZATION OF MANAGEMENT PRINCIPLES (1900-1911)

Gantt's Bonus Plan

Before March 1901, Taylor and his associates' efforts at Bethlehem had mainly been to find out what could be done. The systematizing of the yard labor was an accomplishment, but it did not help to increase the output in the machine shop. In fact this type of work moved slowly as far as results were concerned and in order to speed up production, something drastic had to be done.

In this dilemma, Gantt's plan to pay the men a bonus as an inducement to get their cooperation was a welcome solution. Gantt leaned more toward compromise and conciliation. In his place he combined Halsey's conciliatory idea of a basic day wage with Taylor's idea of a high reward for a large task.

Gantt's plan first called for the payment of a bonus of 50 cents to each workman who had completed all the work assigned him on his instruction card for that day. This plan was adopted and put into practice about the end of March, 1901, and was first applied to the roughing lathes. Less than two months later, R. J. Snyder, then assistant superintendent of the machine shop, in a report made the following comment on the results obtained:

"Mr. E. P. Earle.
Supt. of Machine Shop No. 2

Dear Sir:

I hand you herewith some notes on the results obtained by the introduction of the 'bonus' plan for remunerating labor in

No. 2 machine shop. (here follow machine numbers and dates when they were started on this plan.)

"One of the best results after a short trial has been the moral effect upon the men. They have had it placed in their power to earn a very substantial increase in wages by a corresponding increase in their productive capacity, and this has given them the feeling that the company is quite willing to reward the increased effort. They display a willingness to work right up to their capacity, with the knowledge that they were not given impossibilities to perform. This effect has been brought about by the good use of our excellent slide rules in the hands of a number of the most thoroughly practical men, who, when the results which they demand have been declared impossible to obtain, have repeatedly gone out into the shop and themselves demonstrated that the time was ample, by doing the work well within the limits set. All this has inspired the confidence of the shop hands, and the excellent instruction cards sent out are gradually evolving from laborers a most efficient lot of machine hands . . . The percentage of errors in machining has been very materially reduced, which is unquestionably due to the fact that in order to earn his bonus a man must utilize his brains and faculties to the fullest extent, and so has his attention closely fixed on the work before him, as every move must be made to count. He thus has not time for dreaming, which was, no doubt, the cause of many errors.

"The condition of the machines is vastly improved. Most care has been taken to point out to the men that the best results can be obtained only by keeping their machines in good running condition, well-lubricated and cleaned. They have not been slow to realize this, and cases of journals cutting fast are very rare, while before the introduction of the 'bonus' plan this was a very common occurrence. Breakdowns are also of less frequent occurrence.

"The crane service lately has given us little trouble, and lack of crane service was formerly a constant excuse of the bosses and men for not being able to keep machines filled with work. The improvement in this case arose from the rule laid down that no exceptions or allowances would be made for delays due to this cause.

"It is only by the introduction of this 'bonus' plan that we have had furnished the automatic incentive for men to work up to their capacity and to obtain from the machines the product which they are capable of turning out. It has lifted the hands of the speed bosses (foremen) and enabled them to act in the capacity for which those positions were created—that of instructors.

"These are some of the direct results obtained. Indirectly it has eliminated the constant necessity for driving the men, and has enabled the shop management to divert some of its energy into perfecting the organization, which only will enable us to give a good account of the shop equipment. Much good has also resulted from putting the work through in lots, and keeping each machine as nearly as possible on the same kind of work.

"It is also a pleasure to note in this connection the deep in-interest taken in the work by the men connected with it, and the fine co-operative spirit which prevails among all hands."[1]

It was then suggested to Gantt that an additional bonus be paid to the foreman, if all his men earned their bonuses. As finally adopted, the foreman received a bonus for each man under him who had earned his bonus.

Thus, an adequate incentive was not only given "to the workmen but to the foremen as well." On this new feature Gantt wrote: "This is the first recorded attempt to make it to the financial interest of the fore-man to teach the individual worker, and the importance of it cannot be over-estimated, for it changes the foreman from a driver of his men to their friend and helper."[2]

In December 1901, Gantt presented the ideas and principles of his task and bonus plan to the American Society of Mechanical Engineers in a paper read before their annual meeting. He presented the aims of his system as "an attempt to harmonize the interests of the employer and employee, and, while it affords substantial justice to the employee, requires that he shall always conform to the best interests of his employer."[3]

---

1. H. L., Gantt,, Work, Wages, and Profits, 2nd ed. rev. and enl. New York, 1919, pp. 108-109, the complete report can also be found in: Alford, L. P., Henry, Laurence Gantt Leader in Industry, New York and London, 1934, pp. 88-90.
2. Ibid, p. 115.
3. Transactions, A. S. M. E., Vol. XXIII (1901-1902), p. 341.

He then explained how its application had changed the whole atmosphere within a very short time. The basis of the system is otherwise substantially similar to Taylor's differential piece-rate.

The payment of bonus depends on the fulfillment of two conditions: (1) the work must be satisfactory, and (2) the work must be finished on time. For this reason Gantt believes that "This method is really a system of education with prizes for those who learn . . . ."[1] Compensation, as under the differential system, is quite large for the maximum output of work, while the extra bonus given to the foremen when all their men complete the task "is a strong inducement to make them teach their inferior men."[2] It may have been a practical necessity at Bethlehem to give the foremen this special bonus to get their full cooperation. Since it would be impossible for the men to earn the bonus during a breakdown, this plan quite obviously helped to avoid such breakdowns.

On the basis of his system, Gantt stated that it is not something new but was based on Taylor's system of elementary rate fixing. However, he also claimed it could be used and introduced with greater ease in places where piece-rates would be impossible.

In his paper Gantt explained what he understood the scientific method to be, namely, an analysis of a more or less complicated operation into its elements, and finally, a synthesis, or putting together of the results of such study.

Under the results obtained Gantt mentioned a very large increase in output "averaging from 200 to 300 per cent,"[3] a decrease in accidents and breakdowns, and a quickening of the intelligence of the men.

---

1. Transactions, Vol. XXIII, p. 342.
2. Ibid, p. 343.
3. Ibid, p. 354.

He claims the same advantages for his bonus as Taylor did for the differential piece-rate, namely, that the demoralizing effect of cutting piece-rates is avoided.

Taylor gave due recognition to Gantt's achievement. His comment was as follows:

"Task work with a bonus was invented by Mr. H. L. Gantt, while he was assisting the writer in organizing the Bethlehem Steel Company. The possibilities of his system were immediately recognized by all of the leading men engaged on the work, and long before it would have been practicable to use the differential rate, work was started under this plan. It was successful from the start, and steadily grew in volume and in favor, and to-day is more extensively used than ever before.

"Mr. Gantt's system is especially useful during the difficult and delicate period of transition from the slow pace of ordinary day work to the high speed which is the leading characteristic of good management. During this period of transition in the past a time was always reached when a sudden long leap was taken from improved day work to some form of piece work; and in making this jump many good men inevitably fell and were lost from the procession. Mr. Gantt's system bridges over this difficult stretch and enables the workman to go smoothly and with gradually accelerated speed from the slower pace of improved day work to the high speed of the new system."[1]

Gantt's Graphical Chart.

In spite of all the improvements Taylor introduced, he apparently never succeeeded in getting full cooperation from Linderman, then president of the Bethlehem Steel Company, or from its directors. They were, however, liberal in that they allowed Taylor to make many experiments and spend money on them. On the other hand, he encountered much difficulty in getting the directors to accept the principle of "exceptional wages for exceptional work." He made many appeals not only for the assistants he had brought in, but for those who had been with the company

1. F. W. Taylor, Shop Management, p. 77.

for some time before he had arrived. "These appeals were not entirely in vain. Barth's salary, for example, was raised five hundred dollars a year, which brought it back to what it had been when he left Sellers. But what was accomplished came with a struggle."[1]

Whatever may have been the cause, he left Bethlehem on May 1, 1901.

After leaving Bethlehem Taylor returned to Germantown and was asked by William Sellers to complete the metal cutting investigations in his shop. He listened to Taylor's argument to give scientific management a trial so as to be able to take full advantage of the discovery of high-speed steel and the slide rule. With the idea of introducing scientific management, Taylor suggested that Carl Barth be employed at the Sellers plant.

Barth began his work in November of 1901. Sellers was 77 years old and left the management of his plant to a superintendent who had little understanding or sympathy for Taylor's methods. In addition, he did not seem to have made any attempt at cooperation but at times had serious differences with Barth. Whatever the trouble may have been, Barth did not succeed in introducing the Taylor system at the Sellers' plant despite Sellers' willingness that it be done. He left there early in 1903.

Gantt had left Bethlehem in September 1901 and began his career as a consultant in "modern industrial management." His first job was with the American Locomotive Company, where he began work in January 1902. From there he went to the Robins Conveying Belt Company, then the Brighton Mills, Williamson Brothers Company, the Portland Company, and the Tabor Manufacturing Company.

---

1. Frank Barkley Copley, Frederick W. Taylor, Father of Scientific Management. New York and London: Harper and Brothers, 1923, Vol. 2, p. 141.

At his first job, the American Locomotive Company, he changed his bonus system so as to adjust it for more permanent use. In its new form it had an added feature of giving all the workers a daily rate. Those who finished their tasks in the time set, or less, however, were paid for the number of hours allowed for the tasks plus a certain percentage of that time; for instance, four hours pay for a three hours task. This number of hours pay was then to be given for the work, whether finished in standard time or less. For the worker who was able to accomplish his task or more, this method of payment was the equivalent to piece-work.

In the Spring of 1903, Gantt read another paper before the American Society of Mechanical Engineers on "A Graphical Daily Balance in Manufacture."[1] He felt that in his first paper he had given insufficient information on the method of operating his bonus system, and regarded this new paper simply as a part of "A Bonus System of Rewarding Labor."

In this paper Gantt emphasized that in order to operate the system of bonus payments properly "we must not only have an exact record of what each workman does every day in order to find out whether he has earned his bonus or not, but must have beforehand an exact knowledge of the work to be done and how it is to be done. This amounts to keeping two sets of balances, one of what each workman should do and did do; the other of the amount of work to be done and is done."[2] Gantt calls the former a record concerned with the payment of the bonus. The latter he calls the Daily Balance of Work on each order. This Daily Balance of Work should show at a glance each day what has been done and what remains to be done, thus enabling them "to lay out the work for the next day in the most economical manner." The important point to be considered,

---

1. Transactions of the A. S. M. E., Vol. 24 (1902-1903), pp. 1322-1336.
2. Ibid, p. 1323.

however, is the ease with which such information is available, and
this is greatest when we have it in graphical form. For this reason
he devised a combined schedule of work and balance sheet, most of which
was in the form of a graph.

In a similar way a "balance sheet" for the machine shop and a
routine sheet were made up by Gantt.

Under this system "it is an entirely feasible thing to know
exactly all that has been done in a large plant one day before noon
of the next, and to get a complete balance of work in order to lay
out that afternoon in a logical manner the work for the next day."[1]
While Gantt already used some forms of daily reports at Bethlehem,
The Daily Graphical Balance, as presented in this paper, was primarily
based on his work at the American Locomotive Company where the system,
according to authoritative statements had "worked exceedingly well,"
after being in use for several months. It was probably the beginning
of what would later become the "Gantt Chart."

That Gantt regarded it as part of his bonus system is further sub-
stantiated in his later book on "Work, Wages, and Profits," where he
said: "In installing such a set of schedules the work must be done in
the manner best adapted to the application of the task and bonus system
later."[2] It was no doubt an important step forward, since after standardizing the work and setting the task, the method of control was also
becoming standardized.

Work of Other Leaders.

In June 1903, Taylor presented his paper "Shop Management" before

1. Transactions of the A. S. M. E., Vol. 24 (1902-1903), p. 1330.
2. H. L. Gantt, Work, Wages, and Profits, pp. 269-270.

the annual meeting of the A. S. M. E. at Saratoga. Henry R. Towne hailed it as constituting, in effect, the foundation of a new science, "The Science of Industrial Management."

In summing up the contents of the paper it is safe to say that it was the first complete statement of scientific management principles and practice as conceived by Frederick W. Taylor and the group around him. A movement which began about 1880 and had been developing rather quietly in the shop, was brought to the attention of a wider public and especially to those who were primarily to be affected by the movement and knew its full implications.

Secondly, the differential rate was not to be regarded as an absolute and necessary part of scientific management, but a wider view was to be taken.

Thirdly, we find in this statement of principles a clear and concise exposition of "functional management," the separation of planning from performing, each function to be attended by a foreman who was especially trained for that function, thus leading to further specialization.

"In 'Shop Management' Taylor set up rules and standards comparable to those of a profession and indicated one of the most important steps toward professional management. These principles as set up by Taylor were by no means complete and in time were modified and more 'democraoised.' But they were sufficient at the time and many of them were carried far into the future.

Having formulated his principles and practice of management, Taylor was anxious to get an opportunity to more fully develop his system and demonstrate its workability.

The first opportunity came when Wilfred Lewis, a boyhood chum of Taylor's, was a leading engineer at the Tabor Manufacturing Company.

This company was the principal producer of moulding machines. Along with increasing business, the Tabor Manufacturing Company showed increasing losses. Finally, there was a strike for higher wages and shorter working hours. Lewis came to Taylor for money for the Company, which Taylor advanced willingly. But when Lewis approached him for the second time, Taylor stipulated that the Tabor Company adopt his system of management. In January 1903 Taylor sent Barth to the Tabor Manufacturing Company. There Barth made slide rules for the machines for three and one half months. For the introduction of scientific management principles, Taylor assumed the responsibility himself.

After Taylor had prepared his paper on "Shop Management" but before reading it, he had given advance sheets to James Mapes Dodge, then (1903) president of the A. S. M. E. and one of the heads of the Link Belt Company of Nicetown, Philadelphia. Dodge was an inventor of belts with detachable links for the transmission of power. It is said that his interest in scientific management began with the invention of high-speed steel. As a result of this invention he began to speed up all machines at the Link Belt plant to double the speeds on the line shafts, etc., in order to drive the machine tools to the limit of the tool steel capacity. Output was thus increased but breakdowns occurred which caused these expenses to outweigh the advantage of added output. In this calamity, he consulted Taylor who suggested that the company employ Carl Barth. Hence, when Barth left the Tabor plant in May 1903, leaving the work entirely to Taylor, he went directly to the Link Belt works. It was here that Horace K. Hathaway was employed as an assistant to Barth. Hathaway became so efficient that he finally was loaned to the Tabor Manufacturing Company where he remained permanently, taking full charge except for occasional help from Taylor or Barth.

At the Link Belt Company, and especially at the Tabor Manufacturing Company, Taylor was able to strive openly and conscientiously toward that complete change in mental attitude which he had always regarded as the cornerstone of all the physical changes to be brought about. In trying such a thoroughgoing change, opposition was sure to occur. Very often the system would not work and Taylor had to appeal directly to the company's chief executives.

While the work at the Link Belt Company and the Tabor Manufacturing Company was being done with the cooperation of Taylor and, to a great extent, under his direct supervision, Gantt was doing work of his own. Late in 1903, K. F. Wood, superintendent of the Sayles Bleacheries, Saylesville, Rhode Island, had written to Taylor in regard to some efficiency work at his plant. The latter recommended Gantt.

Gantt's work at Saylesville, broadly speaking, covered the whole field of shop management. He introduced time study and established rates, developed a planning department, and then began to set tasks and pay bonuses. He also installed store control and a cost system, made extensive use of symbols for the different departments, materials, supplies, etc. In doing all this work he broke up the control exercised by the foremen by dividing their work into several functions.

Gantt used much of his experience at Saylesville in his writings, especially in his "Work, Wages, and Profits." It is interesting to note that the organization of these bleacheries down to the present time have remained essentially the way Gantt left them.

It was in December 1908 that Gantt read his paper on "Training Workmen in Habits of Industry and Cooperation." It met with great approval, especially on the gound of being "in harmony with humanitarian

ideas." Such men as William Kent, Dr. Alex C. Humphreys and Charles
Pies valued it very highly. In this paper Gantt maintained that "habits
of industry are far more valuable than any kind of knowledge and skill."

No doubt, Gantt was looking into the future when he prepared his
paper. It is only since the World War that the question has been given
the attention it demands. How great was the influence of Gantt's paper
is debatable. Employee training grew, especially during 1917 and 1918.
Alford wrote: "It is possible, in its final effect upon American industrial practice, that this paper of Gantt's had a more far-reaching
effect than any other of his contributions. Such situations are difficult to evaluate. But this is true, that the training of workmen as it
was developed within a decade after the presentation of this paper has
become an integral part of the management practice in American industry."[1]

Gantt also did valuable work at the Brighton Mills, first in 1906-
1907, and then again in 1909-1910. During the latter period he departed
from the strict adherence to the "Taylor System" in his introduction of
planning and routing. By 1910 "a thorough cost analysis based on factors
was under way."[2]

In the same year Gantt began his most successful work at the Remington Typewriter Company. The Remington Typewriter Company at that
time had 5,000 workers in five factories situated in two different states.
Here Gantt mellowed in his attitude toward business relations, which
improved the technic of installing his methods. As Alford stated:

> "Two of the fundamental policies adopted when he took
> the managership of the Remington plants were: First that
> he would discharge no one if that act could possibly be
> avoided, and that he would allow no one to persuade him to
> take such a course; second, that he would secure the support

---

1. L. P. Alford, "Henry Laurence Gantt Leader in Industry." New York
    and London: Harper and Brothers, 1934, p. 142.
2. Ibid, p. 145.

not only of the officers of his own company, but also of his subordinates and assistants before taking any important step."[1]

This was something new for Gantt after the fights he had at Saylesville, and it was not surprising to see clashes occasionally occur. Before he had used forceful presentation in having his methods accepted. Here, he found that his ideas were more quickly accepted by appealing to the interest of the man involved.

Gantt's work at the Remington Company consisted of planning of method, procedure and performance. He had no administrative responsibilities. His work was no easy task since the factories were producing almost 500 distinct typewriters. Each typewriter contained at that time about 2,500 different parts. First he devoted his time to the control of operating procedure, then he studied and improved sections where the flow of production did not keep up with the rest of the plant. He introduced task and bonus wherever possible and in the planning department, extended his system of graphs by developing a cost and production chart, showing the cost of material and operation. The major results of almost seven years of work were these:[2]

1. The invested capital had been reduced relative to the volume of product. This was brought about by reduction in raw materials and work in process. Other factors were the sale of one plant, a reduction in the number of machine tools and amount of manufacturing equipment required.

2. Factory production had been increased in proportion of 100 to 164. To accomplish this only a few manufacturing machines had been added. The number of working hours had been decreased from 59 to 50 and ten

---

1. L. P. Alford, "Henry Lawrence Gantt Leader in Industry," pp. 160-161, summarized.
2. Ibid, pp. 160-161, summarized.

minute rest periods were introduced for each half day. The number of
employees per unit of product had also decreased.

3. Wages had been increased in the proportion of 100 to 123. At the
same time there had been an average saving of 18 per cent in one
factory on labor cost of the jobs studied and placed on task and bonus.

4. The average labor cost had been reduced in the proportion of 100
to 80. In the largest factory time study and bonus at the close of
1916 had been applied to 3,607 different jobs. Production on these
jobs had increased 65.5 per cent and average wages 24 per cent.

5. The quality of the product was improved.

6. Training of executives and employees for their respective duties
has been done.

7. A spirit of cooperation and goodwill had been cultivated from top
to bottom and the executives were relieved from the supervision of
routine affairs and were made free to deal with exceptional matters
only.

In 1904 Barth read his paper before the American Society of
Mechanical Engineers on a "Slide Rule for the Machine Shop as Part
of the Taylor System of Management." As we are already acquainted
with this subject, we shall only mention the more important factors.
First: Barth mentioned the different variables which "enter into the
problem of determining the most economical way in which to remove a
required amount of stock from a piece of lathe work,"[1] all of which
were now incorporated in his slide rule with the exception of the last
one dealing with "the stiffness of the work." He explained the basis
of the slide rule in presenting algebraic formulas and then went on to
explain the different slide rules made to date, one for the machine

---

1. Transactions of the A. S. M. E., Vol. 25, 1904, p. 50.

shop, to determine feed and speed, and the time slide rule, "this slide will determine the time it will take the tools to traverse the work to the extent wanted."[1] He further mentioned a speed slide rule and the "gear slide rule" designed by Barth, but based on the formulas establish- ed by Wilfred Lewis. Another slide rule he made was to determine the pulling power of belts. The result of the application of these slide rules in one shop was that the superintendent who had "previously worried a good deal about how to get the great amount of work on hand for lathes out of the way, suddenly found himself confronted with a real difficulty in keeping them supplied."[2]

The subject is also of importance and interest because it shows what an important contribution in addition to high-speed steel Barth's slide rules were to scientific management in the machine shop. In judging the results of scientific management, it is, of course, rather difficult to place the right influence or weight on each of the factors involved.

Early Educational Recognition of the Management Movement.

At the annual meeting of the American Society of Mechanical Engi- neers in December 1905, Taylor was elected president.

Soon after the election he heard that the reason for this appoint- ment was the fact that the Society needed reorganization. To help him in his work, Taylor employed Morris Llewellyn Cooke at his own expense. The latter was a graduate of the Engineering School of Lehigh University and met Taylor in 1903. After his meeting with Taylor, Cooke had done

1. Transactions of the A. S. M. E., Vol. 25, 1904, p. 58.
2. Ibid, pp. 61-62.

much work in connection with applying the principles of scientific management to the printing and publishing business and to the office.

Cooke began his work by analysing the functions of the Society and
classifying and standardizing them. He cut the cost of distributing the
annual volume of the Society almost in half. He also founded the Journal
of Proceedings to take the place of the old method according to which
papers accepted by members were printed separately and mailed to the
members prior to each meeting.

In this whole reorganisation, Taylor's main object was to place the
administration of the Society on a strictly business basis.

In 1906 Taylor received the honorary degree of Sc. D. at the dedica-
tion of the new engineering building of the University of Pennsylvania.
As President of the American Society of Mechanical Engineers, he was required to give an address which was later printed and caused much comment.
In it he criticised educational methods in general and engineering education in particular.

In November 1907, Taylor was asked to serve on the Visiting Committee
for Engineers by Professor Ira N. Hollis of Harvard University, Division
of Engineering, as a result of which he received many requests to deliver
addresses at various institutions. In spite of his connections with and
many friends at Harvard University, he strongly opposed the method of
management used at the University, claiming that it was almost a century
old. In 1909, at the request of Henry S. Pritchett, president of the
Carnegie Foundation for the Advancement of Teaching, Taylor recommended
Cooke to make "an economic study of education in this country so far as
the administration of educational work is concerned." Cooke's report on
"Academic and Industrial Efficiency" was published by the Carnegie

Foundation in 1910. In it he made recommendations on financial and business relations of universities and applied many scientific management principles to the University's educational system.

In 1908, Taylor delivered an address before the Harvard Engineering Society of New York, in which he recommended that a college student be "handed over, at the end of his freshman or sophomore year, for a period of from six months to a year, to some commercial or manufacturing establishment."[1] Taylor learned from manufacturers that technical graduates were too theoretical and therefore not fitted to hold executive positions in business. In the same year Taylor was invited to visit the College of Engineering in the University of Cincinnati. This college gave six year courses which required that a student alternately work at a mechanical, chemical or electrical factory in Cincinnati and at the College of Engineering. This was equivalent to three years of actual work in a shop. Taylor felt this was unnecessary.

Shortly thereafter, Taylor gave another address before the Society for the Promotion of Engineering Education. This speech was again significant and reads in part as follows: "... Character comes first; common sense second, and intellectual training third."[2] To accomplish this, Taylor again advocated a plan under which students would be required to work in a shop.

Another factor which Taylor dealt with in his address was "that the great raw material with which more than half of the successful graduates of our technical schools have to deal, receives not a single hour of study at our colleges and university..."[3] By "the great

---

1. Transactions of the A. S. M. E., Vol. 25, 1904, p. 68.
2. Ibid, p. 74.
3. Ibid, p. 78.

raw material," Taylor meant the working man. To this factor, scientific management gave its full attention.

To Taylor's home, "Boxly," in Philadelphia, came an increasing number of people during the succeeding years, to consult with him on all types of management problems.

His talks at Boxly now became part of his campaign for the promotion of scientific management and gradually became improved and "standardized." In addition to business people, professors who were interested in Taylor's scientific management, came to Boxly. Among them were Dean Wallace C. Sabine of the Harvard Graduate School of Applied Science, and Professor Edwin F. Gay of the Division of Economics. After such a visit at Boxly, Gay enlisted Taylor's support to teach the Taylor System "as the final work in management" at Harvard University. This took place in September 1908, when the Harvard Graduate School of Business Administration was opened with Edwin F. Gay as its Dean. Taylor at first was opposed to the idea, maintaining that his system could only be taught in the shop, but he finally consented when Gay threatened to teach scientific management "with or without any help from you." Later, Gay obtained the support of Barth, Hathaway, Cooke and Sanford E. Thompson. Thus, the Harvard Business School was the first to teach Scientific Management.

It was not surprising to find that Taylor was constantly receiving invitations to speak. His address on "Success," prepared with infinite care, was the result of an invitation from the College of Engineering of the University of Illinois. As Copley stated, "his lecture was made up of exact rules and clearly defined principles, illustrated in the concrete with a running series of anecdotes; the whole being served hot

89

from the griddle of life; his own life mostly, though that was conceal-
ed."[1]

In 1909, Taylor, though he was more interested in speaking before
schools on engineering, prepared three lectures for Harvard University.
He improved these lectures and repeated them up through 1914. These
lectures were given free of charge and Taylor refused to be reimbursed
for traveling expenses on his lecture tours.

It may be of interest to note that in this connection management
was taught by the Amos Tuck School of Administration and Finance at
Dartmouth College as early as 1905. This school, in 1910, made Scientific
Management the basic element of its management course. This was done
under the direction of Dr. Harlow S. Person, who maintained "that the
Taylor System was the only system of management which was coherent and
logical, and therefore WAS teachable." Not until 1907, however, did the
American Society of Mechanical Engineers officially recognize management
engineering.

Publicity Attained From the Eastern Rate Case.

Until 1910, scientific management was given little publicity outside the shops where it was tried and installed, and the rather limited
circle of friends and admirers who had been following Taylor's activities.
Scientific Management may have received some publicity through Taylor's
efforts and through the publication of papers in the Transactions of the
American Society of Mechanical Engineers. But little, if anything, was
brought before the general public.

---

1. F. B. Copley, Frederick W. Taylor, Father of Scientific Management,
    Vol. 2, p. 283.

In 1910 the Eastern railroads asked permission of the Interstate Commerce Commission to increase freight rates. At that time Louis D. Brandeis was well-known as "the people's lawyer," defending causes where vital public and human interests were concerned for which he refused any fee. In the case of the railroads, Brandeis offered his services to the shippers to prevent an arbitrary increase in rates. On September 10, 1910 he took the case as counsel for the executive traffic committee of the Eastern Commercial Organization which comprised such organizations as the Baltimore Merchants and Manufacturers' Association, the Boston Chamber of Commerce the Chamber of Commerce of the State of New York, the Fitchburgh (Mass.) Board of Trade and Merchants Association, The New England Shoe and Leather Association, the Newark Board of Trade, the New Haven Chamber of Commerce, the Merchants Association of New York, the Philadelphia Chamber of Commerce, and others — a total of twenty-three associations in all.

Brandeis was a great liberal. When he took up the cause against the roads, it was certainly not against labor.

Brandeis based his whole objection to an increase in rates on the lack of efficiency in railroad management. He was shocked at the lack of accurate information which the railroads had in regard to "the elements of cost entering into the service," and as the hearings in the case proceeded, he was more and more convinced that the lack of net income, of which the railroads complained, was due to "lack of efficiency and of an intimate knowledge of the cost of operation which in competitive industrial businesses had been developed."[1]

---

1. Ibid, p. 370.

Brandeis had previously met Emerson,[1] and discussed problems in efficiency with him. Emerson advised him to see Taylor.

After many meetings with Taylor, Brandeis came in contact with Gantt, Cooke, Barth, Hathaway, Dodge, Towne, and many others identified with the movement. At a conference held in October 1910, the question arose as to what name should be given the management movement in speaking of it at the hearings. It was decided that it be called "scientific management." Conferences of this group representing the scientific management movement were held several times before the hearing at and during the time they were called upon to testify.

In the brief submitted by Brandeis on behalf of the Traffic Committee of Commercial Organizations of the Atlantic Seaboard, the evidence contained therein was chiefly furnished by Emerson. It dealt with scientific management; what it consists of; what it demands; economies brought about through its practical application; and particularly that it does not involve large capital expenditures. In an appeal for cooperation between the roads, he pointed out that railroads do not operate under competitive conditions such as are found in private industry; hence, statistics could be greatly improved upon and made available for other roads. He also brought out the problems of automatic and mechanical improvements which the railroads had not yet studied sufficiently.

Hathaway[2] was the first of the group connected with scientific management to be called upon to testify, which he did very ably.

The testimony as given by Hathaway was the strongest argument which Brandeis used in showing the importance of scientific management and the

---

1. H. Emerson, author of "The Twelve Principles of Efficiency."
2. K. K. Hathaway, author of "Maintenance of Machinery and Equipment as a Part of the Taylor System of Management."

efficiency attainable under it. Output had increased three times without any increase in the size of the plant or any additional floor space. At the same time the number of workmen had been reduced. The management had been fully functionalized and was under complete control, which control rested in the planning department. This was probably the most concrete demonstration of the whole scientific management movement and its practical application.

The next man to testify after Hathaway was James M. Dodge, who at that time was Chairman of the Board of Directors of the Link Belt Company. His company was much larger in size than the Tabor Manufacturing Company and had from 1,800 to 3,000 workers employed in the plants and from 400 to 500 men working on the outside. Dodge testified his plant "was certainly twice as efficient as it was before we used high-speed steel and scientific management."

Other testimony favoring the cause of scientific management was given by Frank B. Gilbreth. His testimony was hailed as of special importance because it seemed to prove that scientific management could be successfully applied to union labor. Gilbreth had once been a member of the Boston Bricklayers Union. Later he became contracting engineer. As such, he did not like to pay piece-rates, but finally overcame his scruples by guaranteeing the men a day-rate, and paying a bonus once the workman reached a certain standard of output.

Charles B. Going, editor and publisher of the Engineering Magazine, testified that he had made a personal investigation of the work done at Santa Fe by Emerson. He had found the existence of functional organization in the locomotive repair shops and to some extent in the freight car repair shops. He had seen time studies being made and had seen the standard schedules and standard instruction cards in use. He had spent five weeks in this investigation on Emerson's work.[1]

Robert Thurston Kent, editor and publisher of Industrial Engineering and a graduate of Stevens Institute, had been at the Link Belt plant during 1903 and 1904. He gave testimony to the effect that the men at the Link Belt plant liked to work under scientific management; that they were chiefly interested in the amount of money they earned. Kent had also visited some shops of the Canadian Pacific where scientific management had been partially introduced. It is interesting to note in this connection that the work of proper routing, scheduling and dispatching in the case of railroads had been of even greater importance than standardisation or bonus payments and very often resulted in increased production of from 30 to 40 per cent, while in other instances, output had been practically doubled.

The Commission decided against the railroads.

The effects of the rate case hearings were felt immediately. Daily papers and periodicals carried series of articles explaining scientific management. Addresses were given throughout the country, especially at colleges. The Amos Tuck School of Dartmouth College held conferences on this subject. The discussions at Dartmouth were later published. A general movement was under way to give courses on scientific management at colleges. Harvard has already been mentioned. Courses were now given at Dartmouth, the Polytechnic Institute of Brooklyn, Purdue University, and the Universities of Maine, Minnesota, Missouri and Wisconsin. Yale introduced similar courses.

At other colleges and universities part of the literature on scientific management was introduced into courses in economics or engineering.

---

1. Eastern Rate Case Hearings, p. 2821.

Scientific management was suddenly pushed into the front and constituted, from a practical and theoretical point of view, one of the most important problems of the industrial world. Scientific management and efficiency became public property and the increase in literature on the subject of "efficiency" is very significant in showing the influence of the rate hearings. A table showing the sudden increase is given on this page.

While scientific management was thus made public property, opposition by labor increased, especially organised labor, which saw its most deadly enemy in the movement now under way. In the plants where scientific management had been introduced, organised labor was not strong enough to throw its full force behind the opposition. But it soon had its opportunity in the government service. The following table indicates increasing interest on the subject:

All Periodical Articles on Efficiency Subjects[1]

1907 8		1910 15
1908 5		1911 59
1909 7		1912 38

Taylor had become associated with Admiral Caspar F. Goodrich through the Manufacturing Investment Company and the two had always kept in close touch with each other. Hence, when Goodrich, in 1907, was ordered to command the Brooklyn Navy Yard he at once conferred with his superior, Truman H. Newberry, Assistant Secretary of the Navy (later to become secretary), and advised him about the conditions at the navy yards. He

---

1. "Select list of references on scientific management and efficiency" see "Efficiency Number" compiled under the direction of H.H.B. Meyer, chief bibliographer, Library of Congress, as part of Special Libraries, May 1913. See also Drury, H. B., Scientific Management, New York 1922, p. 41 (Revised and Enl. edition).

also asked Newberry whether recommendations from him would be considered favorable. After having received positive assurances to this effect, he began to reorganize the whole set-up of the yard. In connection with this work, Goodrich very often conferred with Taylor before taking any final step. Of more importance, however, is the fact that each change, after its trial in Brooklyn, was immediately enforced at all other navy yards.

One of the outstanding events was the concentration of all tool making for the Atlantic navy yards at League Island. This tool making shop was organized under the direction of Hathaway. Barth was also brought in for a very short time at the Booklyn Navy Yard. Politics and the change in administration, however, put a definite limit to the improvements at the Navy Yard.

In 1908, but independent of what was being done in Brooklyn and on the Atlantic Seaboard, Holden A. Evans, a naval instructor, started to reorganize the work at Mare Island in California soon after his appointment as constructor in charge of that Island. Evans had been greatly impressed by Taylor's "Shop Management," and put his principles of scientific management into practice. He seemed to have had a great degree of independence and success due to the fact that he was three thousand miles away from Washington. His success in increasing the output of the shop led him to write to Taylor (1906) describing his results and asking for further information. Although labor was much more expensive on the Pacific Coast, Evans finally reduced labor costs at Mare Island to below those in any eastern yard. In 1909 the Federal Administration changed and George Von L. Meyer became the new Secretary of Navy. Under him most of the improvements made in the navy yards were gradually undone. Admiral Goodrich, guessing the outcome, retired to

private life. Evans was able to continue for more than a year but was
finally transferred and completely failed in his efforts to get scientific
management reestablished in the navy yards. He finally asked for a leave
of absence without pay for one year in order to give all his time to the
study of scientific management so that he could better serve the navy.
This was denied him and in a short time he was transferred to the Atlantic
Coast. His last place was the Norfolk Navy Yard where he was promised a
free hand for the introduction of "modern management." After having been
there for four days the instructions which had given him a free hand were
cancelled. As a result he resigned immediately (1911) from the Navy and
went into private business to later become general manager of the Baltimore
Dry Docks and Ship Building Company.

Now, that which was discarded in the navy yards was at the same time
being introduced in the ordnance plants of the army. The moving force
behind this development was General William Crozier, Chief of Ordnance.
Crozier had been acquainted with Taylor's work for several years, while
one of his subordinates, Major F. E. Hobbs, had seen the early developments of the Taylor System in the 1880's, when he was stationed at Midvale
as an inspector. In 1908 Hobbs became commanding officer of Rock Island
Arsenal, at Rock Island, Illinois, and immediately attempted to make
time studies and set piece-rates based on them. As a result of objections raised by some of the workmen, political pressure prevented further
efforts in that direction at least until the elections were over.

In the meantime, however, General Crozier had made a visit to Boxly
(January 1909) and to the Tabor and Link Belt plants, where he collected
additional information on the subject. Then he was told that the reason
for Major Hobbs' failure had been primarily due to the introduction of
time study before the men had been properly prepared and before conditions

of machinery, tools and materials had been standardized. After having
learned these facts and having made his own investigation, General
Crozier decided to make a test of the system at the Watertown Arsenal.
He was fully supported by Colonel C. B. Wheeler, commanding officer of
the Arsenal, in his endeavors. Mr. Wheeler, with many of the ordnance
officers, was sent to Boxly to get fully acquainted with the system.
Barth was the first expert to be employed. Later, Dwight D. Merrick
became his assistant and served as time study expert. The Arsenal had
about 600 employees. In May, 1911, Barth's work had advanced sufficiently so that the first bonus could be offered. After two years the
system had advanced so far that about 45 per cent of the work was done
under it in the machine shop. The percentage of work done under the
bonus system in other departments was still low.

The best report on the work is contained in the report of the War
Department for the fiscal year ending June 30, 1912. In this report,
General Crozier gave special attention to the trials made in scientific
management at the Watertown Arsenal. In it he said that scientific
management had saved them $49,000, but if as much of the system had
been in practical use for the whole year as was during the last two
months of the fiscal year, the savings would have been $100,000. Great
reductions had also been made in stores and estimates for the following
year were reduced by $240,000. In 1913, in a memorandum to the Secre-
tary of War, Crozier gave the amounts paid out in premiums and stated
that workers in the machine shop were earning on an average of 24 per
cent more when working on bonus than on the day rate, many earned
from 30 to 35 per cent more, while less than 4 per cent did not earn
their bonuses. The basis of the bonus was set as follows: First,
the time was ascertained in which the work could be done, this time

was then increased by two-thirds, while for every minute saved from the time allowed one-half minute additional pay (bonus) was given. Crozier also stated that up to that time no worker had been discharged for failing to earn the bonus.

The system was later applied to other arsenals, including the one at Rock Island. However, when Taylor's "job card" was introduced at Rock Island (1911), labor agitation began and one of the machinists, N. P. Alifas, took over its leadership.

Organized Opposition of Labor.

The chief issue involved in the extension of scientific management to the government arsenals, was the opposition of organized labor to the scientific management movement. In 1910, General Crozier had formed a board which included the commanding officers of the government manufacturing arsenals. This board made a study of the improvements accomplished at Watertown and recommended their adoption elsewhere. But when the introduction of the system of Rock Island began, it met with vigorous opposition on the part of organized labor. In addition to Alifas, whom we mentioned above and who made himself the direct representative of the employees at Rock Island, President Gompers of the American Federation of Labor and O'Connell, president of the International Association of Machinists, took up the fight against it. In the summer of 1911 an attempt was made to introduce the bonus system into the foundry department of the Watertown Arsenal, as a result of which the whole force walked out. This was probably the result of stiffened opposition. The walk-out did not last very long and the introduction continued thereafter. In April of the same year, O'Connell had sent out a circular to all lodges of the International Association of Machinists. In this circular, scientific management was attacked as the arch-enemy of labor.

Organised labor was resolved to fight. Protests came to the
Secretary of War from the lodges of the Machinists, while a committee
representing Rock Island employees came to Washington to protest. As
a result, a resolution was introduced in Congress directing the Committee on Labor to investigate the Taylor System.

On August 21, 1911, shortly after the strike of the moulders at
Watertown, the House of Representatives adopted a resolution to the
effect that the speaker appoint a committee of three to make an investigation. The members of this committee were W. B. Wilson, who
later became Secretary of Labor, William C. Redfield, who later became Secretary of Commerce, and John Q. Tilson. Wilson had formerly
been an officer in the United Mine Workers. Redfield was a manufacturer
with some experience in scientific management, while Tilson had no experience in anything resembling shop management. These three men now
formed the Special Committee of the House of Representatives. The
hearings were held in Boston, New York and Washington and lasted from
October 4, 1911 to February 12, 1912.

It seemed that Taylor had to do the fighting himself to a great
extent. Private establishments did not want to have the attention of
the labor organisations drawn to them.

In the final report of the Committee to the House which was
unanimous, it stated that:

> "Neither the Taylor system, the Emerson system, the
> Gantt system ...., nor any of the systems of so-called
> scientific management have been in existence long enough
> for your committee to determine with accuracy their effect
> on the health and pay of employees and their effect on
> wages and labor cost. The conclusions we have arrived at
> are all based upon what we consider to be the logical
> sequence of the conditions existing or proposed. The

selection of any system of shop management for the various Government works must be to a great extent a matter of administration, and your committee does not deem it advisable nor expedient to make any recommendations for legislation upon the subject at this time."

Thus it actually failed to find any ground in the representations made by labor leaders upon which to base condemnation or serious criticism of the methods used or their effects in the Government arsenals. Especially important is that no cases of overwork or overspeeding were found, resulting in ill-health among the labor force.

At the annual convention of the American Federation of Labor in 1913, and again in 1914, resolutions were adopted condemning the system. The arguments advanced chiefly dealt with the human side of the problems involved and since the opposition started from the top, it may have been a preventive measure rather than a measure against the damage already done. As far as government service was concerned, the opposition succeeded during these years, but this success did not prevent or retard the spreading of the system in private business.

Increase in Public Interest.

In 1909 Taylor prepared a paper in which the philosophy of management would be more comprehensively dealt with. For this purpose he addressed a member of the Meeting Committee of the A. S. M. E. in order to obtain his reaction on the subject of his new paper. Taylor was encouraged by this gentleman as well as by the secretary of the Society. Hence, in January 1910, he submitted his first draft.

But when the Meeting Committee failed to act on it, he withdrew and rewrote it. After about a year had elapsed, the Committee still had not acted on it. The delay was caused by the avowed policy of the A. S. M. E.

to avoid discussions of controversal subjects in management. In the
meantime, however, the American Magazine and the Atlantic Monthly had
taken an interest in his new paper. Encouraged by some friends who
felt Scientific Management could now be best promoted by placing it
before the general public, Taylor decided (early in 1911) to have it
printed in the American Magazine. He withdrew it formally from the
A. S. M. E., but had a special pamphlet edition printed for distribution
among the members of the Society.

It was thus that his "Principles of Scientific Management" came
before a larger public than any of his previous papers. In 1911 it
appeared in three issues of the magazine, and in 1917 was published
by Harper Brothers. After the Rate Case Hearings and the hearings
before the Special Committee, the public was eager to know more about
the questions involved and the publications were therefore very timely.

In November 1910, a meeting was held at the Athletic Club in New
York to consider the question of forming an organization dealing
primarily with management problems. At this meeting there were such
men present as Morris L. Cooke, Frank B. Gilbreth, Robert Kent, Conrad
Lauer (representing Charles Day) and Wilfred Lewis.[1] On this occasion
it was decided to organize a society for the discussion and promotion
of scientific management. There was no formal organization at this
time, but from then on James M. Dodge presided at the meetings, while
Robert Kent acted as secretary-treasurer. On November 7, 1912, the
society was formally organized and Dodge was elected president and

1. L. P. Alford, Ten Years Progress, in the Transactions of the A. S. M. E.,
   1922, p. 1265.

Kent secretary. The meetings which previously had been held every month were now held less often, but were better planned. The name of the organisation was the "Society to Promote the Science of Management," which was changed to "Taylor Society" after Taylor's death. The purpose of the new group was "to furnish an opportunity for men intensively interested in the principles and practice of Scientific Management, and occupied in installing such management to discuss not only the theories and philosophy of management, but the technic ...."[1]

The year 1911 was marked by an "efficiency movement." This was no easy time for Taylor. He was now in the limelight; was called upon to render his judgment of engineers in various institutions; and had to assume the heavy burden of giving many lectures. But efficiency and what he stood for were two different things. The mental revolution, a change of attitude of employer and employee towards their work and towards each other, was to him part of the system. It is therefore not surprising to find that he always recommended Barth, Gantt, Hathaway or Cooke when his advice was sought for the choice of an engineer.

During this time Brandeis did much to win the labor unions for the cause of scientific management. In an address before the Boston Central Labor Union on April 12, 1911, Brandeis stated that it had been easier "to tap the inexhaustible foreign labor supply than to devise and to introduce better methods and better management. Instead of keeping down the labor cost by eliminating unnecessary human effort and increasing the productivity of the individual, we met the workingman's demand

---

1. L. P. Alford, Ten Years Progress, p. 1286.

for higher wages by increasing the supply of the workers."[1] These
conditions have changed since the social sense of the community had
intervened. Beginning with this, Brandeis explained to his listen-
ers how savings in waste through scientific tests, elimination of
dishonesty, proper methods of storing and accounting could be attained.
Similar savings could be attained in the plant through careful planning
so as to secure its full use. From there on Brandeis went on to explain
scientific management. Scientific management, he stated, is not hostile
to labor. The charge that it was "speeding up" and that it sought to
make the men work harder, thus exhausting the workmen, was not true.
"Such criticism shows a complete misconception of scientific management.
Conserving human effort, and the man, is a fundamental tenet of scientific management."[2] He also said that when Taylor discovered the laws
by which a definite quantity of pig iron might be loaded, or the laws
of shovelling, etc., he was protecting his workmen and not exhausting
them. On the bonus system to which labor also objected he said that
"it is a common incident under scientific management; but it is not to
be supposed that it IS scientific management."[3]

Scientific management may be applied without bonus, the important
thing is that the workman gets a square deal or in other words, A
proper share of the profit which he aids in producing. In practice it
has been found to be the fairest method.

On the question of unionism and collective bargaining, Brandeis
suggested that through the latter minimum wages and bonuses may be
fixed and where bonus payment shall begin or be applied.[4] In the same

1. L. D. Brandeis, Business A Profession, Boston 1914, p. 38. This
   address was also published in the Survey of April 22, 1911.
2. Ibid, p. 41.
3. Ibid, p. 43.
4. Ibid, p. 46.

address he mentioned that scientific management did not create unemployment since it made goods cheaper, through which more could be
bought for the same money. Nor did it displace the inefficient
worker, "on the contrary it helps the 'inefficient' most." It trains
the workmen in habits of industry (Gantt).

In the same year Rudolf Blankenburg was elected Mayor of Philadelphia. Being elected on a reform ticket, he immediately turned to
Taylor urging him to become Director of Public Works. Taylor declined,
but realizing this to be an opportunity to demonstrate some of the
principles in public works for which he was striving, he recommended
Morris L. Cooke for the position. Mr. Cooke accepted and upon assuming
his new duties, he found the Department of Public Works in Philadelphia
about the "worst plant" he had ever been in. He could introduce little
of scientific management, but had to be contented with making ordinary
improvements. A rather outstanding event was his suit against the
Philadelphia Electric Company. This suit brought the city a reduction
of about $150,000 a year in rates, and to private consumers about
$900,000. For his activities in connection with this, Cooke was attack-
ed by representatives of public utility companies in 1914 at a meeting
of the A. S. M. E., but was very ably and forcefully defended by Taylor.

In June of this same year, Fred J. Miller of the Union Typewriter
Company and one of Taylor's most active supporters in the A. S. M. E.,
wrote the latter, cautioning him in his habit of pointing to "soldiering"
as one of the greatest evils among the workmen of today. Miller drew
attention to the fact that the Union of Machine Workers had more than
doubled its membership within a very short time, using as a means to
get the men, statements made by Taylor in articles and addresses. Taylor,

however, held that "the press ought to get busy and teach the people
what this means for the country."[1] Miller in a second letter mentioned how the talk of overproduction strengthened the workmen's belief in
a restriction of output. The idea further found support in the Pro-
tective Tariff and the Wage Fund theories. To this Taylor in his reply
reiterated what he had said in his previous letter where he had mentioned that he felt restriction of output to be the greatest evil which be-
fell present-day England and became a curse on her. But he now added
that he had not met a single workman during the past year with whom he
had t a l k e d, who "did not acknowledge that he was deliberately soldiering in his work." He closed the letter by saying: "Until our news-
papers and magazines take this matter up in earnest I feel that we shall
not be doing our duty towards the working people."[2]

On this question of soldiering and the opposition of organised
labor to scientific management, Harlow S. Person wrote:

"Organised labor had a long and hard struggle to achieve
status in the face of the strong opposition of industry, and
its natural assumption was that anything new originating in
management and by management was for ownership's advantage
and presumably to labor's disadvantage. -- Assertion concerning
the development of a 'science for each operation' and the
reduction of operating methods to easily understood instructions,
caused a fear of the loss to labor of craft distinctions and
the power of labor in the possession of craft knowledge and skill;

"Numerous statements concerning economies which had been
effected by scientific management, especially in the nature of
labor saving, called up at once the instinctive fear that a
general adoption of scientific management would cause widespread discharges and unemployment;

"Inadequate explanations of the use and limitations of
time study, and of reasons for increase of productivity,

---

1. F. B. Copley, Frederick W. Taylor, Father of Scientific Management,
    Vol. 2, p. 408; for full exchange of letters, see pp. 407-409.
2. The Taylor Society, Scientific Management in American Industry, pp. 18-19.

led to an assumption that scientific management means a speeding up, wearing out and eventual casting aside of the individual worker."[1]

This is probably the best statement giving the facts as they really were in 1929. He then added that the oppositon to bona fide scientific management by labor leaders had practically disappeared, while recent years had seen noteworthy cooperation between scientific management leaders and labor leaders.[2]

Again, we must not forget how in these early years, especially after scientific management had received so much publicity, an increasing number of quacks appeared who called themselves "efficiency engineers." In April 1911, Taylor wrote to a friend on this point as follows:

"I am in entire agreement with you that before fall the woods will be full of quacks who are introducing scientific management, and they will be highly likely to give a black eye to the whole movement in many cases. However, enough of the good work will survive to make it continue, and within two or three years the manufacturers throughout the country will be pretty well alive to the necessity of getting first-class men to help them in their reorganisation."[3]

Many manufacturers wrote to Taylor, complaining about the situation. He agreed with them stating as follows:

"I am not at all surprised at the experience you had in the application of scientific management. About 99 out of 100 men who have taken up the profession of introducing scientific management are either plain fakers or men who are merely in the business for the money they can get out of it.

"There are exceedingly few men who have had the large range of experience necessary to make a substantial success of this work."[4]

---

1. The Taylor Society, Scientific Management in American Industry, New York, 1929 (edited by Harlow S. Person), pp. 18-19.
2. Ibid, p. 20.
3. Copley, op. cit., p. 388.
4. Ibid.

In 1912, a paper entitled "The Present State of the Art of
Industrial Management" was placed before the A. S. M. E. This paper
constituted the major report of the Sub-Committee on Administration
and was signed by the following members: J. M. Dodge, as chairman,
L. P. Alford, as secretary, and D. M. Bates, H. A. Evans, Wilfred Lewis,
W. L. Lyall, W. B. Tardy and H. R. Towne, all members.

The report took cognizance of the sudden popular interest in the
subject of industrial management which had become evident even to the
most superficial observer.

The popular interest is further proved, states the report, by the
great number of articles published in the daily papers and popular
magazines which otherwise give scant attention to technical subjects.
There has also been demonstrated a sudden interest in the subject on
the part of employers and business executives, as shown by lectures,
professional papers, and reports presented to their associations. Then
there developed a sudden opposition of labor and statements were issued
by their leaders. The government began its investigation while private
groups began the formation of societies for the furtherance of the
application of scientific management.

On the work accomplished through scientific management, the committee
stated in its report:

"But the most important change and one that comprehends
the others is in the mental attitude toward the problems of
production. The tendency is toward an attitude of questioning,
or research, or careful investigation of everything affecting
the problems on hand, the seeking for exact knowledge and then
shaping action on the discovered facts. It has developed the
use of time study and motion study as instruments for investigation, the planning department as an agency to put into practice
conclusions drawn from the results or research, and methods of
wage payment which stimulate cooperation."[1]

1. Transactions of the A. S. M. E., 1912, p. 1137.

The report also pointed out how this rise in mental attitude could be traced in the different papers presented before the American Society of Mechanical Engineers dealing with the subject of scientific management. These papers, numbering sixteen in all, covered the period from 1886 to 1908, while the practice on which they were based even goes further back.

In its entirety, the report and subsequent discussions show how wide-awake and alert a certain group of men within the A. S. M. E. were to new developments in the field of scientific management. The report in turn served to draw the attention of a still wider group to these developments.

Congressional Hearings on "Efficiency Systems and Labor."

As we have seen, labor opposition had been growing stronger during the past years. As a direct result of the many petitions sent to Congress, the Industrial Relations Commission spent four days in April 1914 taking testimony on scientific management.

The testimony taken during these hearings was not confined to the Taylor System, but the investigation was carried on under the broad term of "Efficiency Systems and Labor." Of the efficiency experts, Taylor was the first called upon to testify.

He spoke on the general principles involved; on the restriction of output in England and the evil of soldiering here; where one of the very first steps of scientific management had been able to correct that evil. He followed with the statement that for thirty years where scientific management had been in practical use, there never had been a strike. Why? "Because the essence of the matter is friendship." In explaining scientific management, he said: ".... under scientific

management the men give their initiative, their goodwill, their hard-
work with absolute regularity."[1] This duty is assumed by the men
voluntarily and it is this assumption of duty by the men which makes
the vast improvements possible.

One of the chief purposes of the hearings was to investigate the
different efficiency systems in regard to their relations with the
working force and the unions. Hence, towards the end of his testimony
Taylor was chiefly queried on questions of labor, with such questions
as: "To whom will the increased earnings mainly go?" "Does it go to the
employer only?" Taylor answered, under the old system, in the affirm-
ative; under the new system: "Not at all, we absolutely safeguard our
men,"[2] meaning thereby that this increased surplus is equally divided
between employer, employee and consumer.

When asked whether the system had been anywhere in operation long
enough to regard it as a permanent condition, Taylor gave this rather
significant answer: "I cannot conceive of any set of American workmen
continuing to stay, as they have, year after year, with one company,
unless they found that they were better treated than anywhere else. I
know that my workmen friends are still at the Midvale Steel Company's
works, and I know also, that the managers of the Midvale Steel Company's
works are the same that I trained and left there many years ago.[3]

When Emerson testified he expressed himself to be in favor of
collective bargaining and for selecting an expert mediator. Standards
can be set high without injustice to anyone so long as day-rates are
guaranteed. On the other hand, he did not dismiss a man unless he was

---

1. Commission on Industrial Relations; Final Report and Testimony.
   Congress 64, 1, Sen. Doc. No. 415, p. 775.
2. Ibid, p. 796.
3. Ibid, p. 796.

only about 30 per cent efficient. If he was 50 per cent efficient
"we thought he was a good promising prospect to bring up to 100 per cent."[1]
No harm was done by making time studies with the stop-watch or otherwise,
if it was done with the full consent of the men. Intelligent workers did
not resent the stop-watch "when it was properly explained to them."

Almost all the rest of his testimony was on his bonus system. On
the basis of his system, Emerson said: "We pay the man for all the time
he saves above 20 per cent; 20 per cent because he did the standard work
for the time he worked; that is our moral basis. The other is the computing basis, but they are the same, they work out just the same."[2]

Among the individuals who testified in the Hearings taken by the
Committee on Industrial Relations was Charles W. Mixter, a graduate of
Johns Hopkins, and a student of Harvard for two years. Mixter professed
to be the first who ever taught scientific management. He was professor
at the University of Vermont for ten years where he taught economics and
scientific management to engineering students. Later he took a leave of
absence and spent one year in the Tabor Manufacturing Company to study
the Taylor System. He then served a sort-of apprenticeship as time study
man and finally became active in installing scientific management. In
his testimony, he gave some of his experiences in scientific management.
He thought that scientific management was a rival organization to the
trade unions who took away their trade. If collective bargaining and
task-setting management has to maintain its prerogative, labor does not
need a representative at the elbow of the time-study man. While he

---

1. Commission on Industrial Relations; Final Report and Testimony.
    Congress 64, 1, Sen. Doc. No. 415, p. 827.
2. Ibid, p. 829.

favored collective bargaining in principle, he stated that if it were applied to the setting of task and bonus, it would only bring delays and friction. Especially is it "impractical to give labor a voice while the system is being installed,"[1] during which time it should be suspended. Have task and bonus installed and let objections come afterwards. While he was generally sympathetic with labor, he stated that his work had now brought him in contact with the difficulties faced by employers.

Although a newcomer to the practical field of scientific management, he was nevertheless taking a distinctly professional attitude towards it, and when asked whether the installer of the system was not primarily employed by the employer he answered: "Yes, to a degree; but with that tempering force that comes always with the professional man. You call in a doctor, and you can not order him to do anything, although you are his employer. He has his standards and ideals of the ethics of his profession, and the same with a lawyer of standing." Hence, from this professional point of view, he was certainly interested in the welfare of the worker.

In the testimony of James M. Dodge, he stressed the increased earnings of the men under scientific management. He was also questioned as to the health of the employees. In answer, Dodge gave some data on time lost through sickness which read as follows: in 1911, it was 1.2 per cent; in 1912, 1.5 per cent; and in 1913, 1.4 per cent time lost by shopmen. The only complaints received were from men who wanted to come under the task and bonus system. Scientific management had greatly increased the stability of the business. "We have established a

---

1. Commission on Industrial Relations; Final Report and Testimony. Congress 64, 1, Sen. Doc. No. 415, p. 834.

stability in our business that we never were able to establish before."[1]

David Van Alstyne, assistant to the president of the New York, New Haven and Hartford Railroad had previously been with many other companies. In the American Locomotive Company he introduced the Emerson System. He had also done betterment-work when he was with the Northern Pacific. At the American Locomotive Company, union and non-union labor were opposed to the system, and after he had left the company threw it out. He testified, however, to the effect that a collective bargaining agreement could be entered into between a labor union and scientific management as follows:

> "I made an agreement with the moulders' and blacksmiths' union which was the ordinary trade agreement but the principle feature of it was that the unions committed themselves to a maximum output, of which the company was to be the judge, and the basis of it was the Emerson standard time system and a bonus paid for efficiency above two-thirds in addition to the straight day's wages ... In order to facilitate matters we agreed to make the standard time by means of a demonstrator, and if there was no objection to that we put the time into effect, and it became the standard; it was provided for in the agreement that the shop committee could object at any time they wanted to, and if the shop officials and the shop committee could not agree, it was further provided that it would be officially settled by me and the head of the union."[2]

Interesting as well as amusing is Carl G. Barth's testimony. It is interesting because much of his early work and connection with scientific management is revealed in it; and amusing because of his peculiar English. A special charm was further lent to his speech by his foreign accent. When asked for a definition of his business, he answered:

> "Well that is an awful hard question to answer, but as people insist that a man assume a title in order to cover a

---

1. Commission on Industrial Relations; Final Report and Testimony. Congress 64, 1, Sen. Doc. No. 415, p. 872.
2. Ibid, p. 884.

multitude of sins, I assumed the title of consulting engineer because I can do anything under the sun under that title."[1]

Under direct questioning, Barth was rather careful in his answers. On the question as to whether the earnings of the laboring man under scientific management would not be reduced in the long run, he said: "It has not run long enough to prove that." With the question of collective bargaining, he did not seem to have been particularly acquainted for he stated in this connection: "As I have never seen collective bargaining, but I have only heard of it, I cannot say anything about it ..."[2]

Sanford E. Thompson was also among those who testified. In his last publication on the "Principles of Scientific Management," Taylor had mentioned him as "perhaps the most experienced man in motion and time study in this country." Thompson was born in 1867 and in 1889 received his degree of B. S. He then became engaged in civil and mechanical engineering. In 1895 he came into closer contact with Taylor and in the following year began his time studies of various jobs in the building trades. These studies continued up to 1902. His time studies included such work as excavation, masonry, bricklaying, concrete and cement work, lathing and plastering, carpentry, slating and roofing, and rock quarrying. His method was to split up the work into its elements or into separate operations. He timed them in hundredths of a minute. In 1905, he published jointly with Taylor, "Concrete, Plain and Reinforced," and in 1911, "Concrete Costs." He had also assisted Taylor at the Symonds Rolling Machine Company where he was in charge of the motion study analysis.

---

1. Commission on Industrial Relations; Final Report and Testimony. Congress 64, 1, Sen. Doc. No. 415, p. 886.
2. Ibid, p. 895.

When asked about the form or method of paying labor, Thompson replied in such a manner as to shed some light on the diversity of methods in existence in actual practice. To him the form of payment was of little fundamental importance compared with the scientific determination of the task.

Thompson did not object to unions but like many of the leaders, thought such unions became an unnecessary adjunct under scientific management. In his practice about half of his time was devoted to the building trade, while the other half was devoted to shops. How manifold his work must have been can be seen from the fact that he was the man who made the original time studies and set the tasks at the Plimpton Press. The only field in which he never had anything to do was the machine shop.

Gantt's testimony before the Committee on Industrial Relations was rather short and covered facts already mentioned, such as his experience at the Brighton Mills. On the assignments of tasks he said: "We are not going to ask anybody to perform a task unless we have entirely satisfied him that that task is an executable one. We do not discriminate against him if he refuses."[1] Gantt also explained his charts and told the Committee that an investigation is made as soon as a worker fails to perform his task, "Scientific management is management by facts and not mere opinion. We have to be able to differentiate between facts and opinions."[2]

For Louis D. Brandeis the science of management "is nothing more than an organised effort, pursued intensively, to eliminate waste."[3]

_____

1. Commission on Industrial Relations; Final Report and Testimony.
   Congress 64, 1, Sen. Doc. No. 415, p. 957.
2. Ibid, p. 957.
3. Ibid, p. 993.

In this effort we need the cooperation of management and labor and therefore "I take it that in order to accomplish this result it is absolutely essential that the unions should be represented in the process."[1] He would then give the labor organization a competent voice in the selection of an expert. Labor should not only have a voice in the determination of the factors involved, but also in ascertaining the facts.

Scientific management in his opinion did not undermine the union. It might have for a time but certainly not in the long run, for "unless the interests of the workingman are protected by his representatives, neither scientific management nor any other method of employment or compensation will protect the laborer."[2] In the fight between scientific management and labor, Brandeis thought that labor leaders as well as experts in scientific management had been at fault. But scientific management will improve conditions and, therefore, to a certain extent mitigate the labor unrest.

A brief review of the testimony given by some of the labor leaders should be noted.

A. J. Berres, then Secretary of the Metal Trades Department of the American Federation of Labor, was told that the burden of proof would rest on him to state to the satisfaction of the Commission that scientific management "does injure men physically." If he would fail in this, his charge would have nothing to stand on. To this Berres replied:

---

1. Commission on Industrial Relations; Final Report and Testimony.
   Congress 64, 1, Sen. Doc. No. 415, p. 993.
2. Ibid, p. 996.

"I think that when a number of men such as the number
I am going to mention, take the position they do, there
might be something radically wrong, and I have every right
to assume what they say is right. If you would take the
Watertown Arsenal today where there are 180 machinists, you
will find the most affected trade by the installation of
so-called efficiency system, where there are over 150 out
of 180 men who would, if they were given the opportunity
tomorrow, repudiate the system; and that, I think, justifies
the commission in making some investigation of those men
themselves. That is the evidence we get.

"Commissioner Weinstock. In other words, you offer those
                    men as your witnesses?

"Mr. Berres. Yes."[1]

While he offered these individuals as witnesses, as it later turned

out, he was unable to actually prove the charge.

N. P. Alifas stated the now-familiar objections raised by labor to

scientific management. He represented District 44 of the International

Association of Machinists which included machinists from the arsenals

and navy yards. His introductory remark was as follows:

"We object to the system of scientific management as
a whole on account of the way it is built up, and we also
have specific objections against certain features of it
to which we would object even though they were segregated
and were acted upon apart from the system as a whole."[2]

In the first instance he felt that it was humiliating to "have a

man hold a stop-watch on us." Then it is also unfair that the employer

should set the pace   He had asked as many as seventy-five machinists as

to whether they would prefer the premium payment or would rather go

back to day work, to which they replied that they would prefer the day

work.[3]

---

1. Commission on Industrial Relations; Final Report and Testimony.
   Congress 64, 1, Sen. Doc. No. 415, p. 909.
2. Ibid, p. 940.
3. Ibid, p. 954.

John Golden, who seemed to have been one of the organizers, stated that the Textile Workers Union had made an investigation at the Brighton Mills. The Mills employed at that time 635 operatives, of which 445 were male and 190 female. They represented about nine or ten nationalities. The employees had to work 58 hours per week. Of those interviewed (men and girls) many had complained that they were driven too much.[1] Some had also said that they disliked the system, "but what can we do about it."

The Hoxie Investigation.

After hearing the testimony of both sides, the commission authorized a more exhaustive study which was carried through in the latter part of 1914 and early part of 1915. The commission first employed Robert F. Hoxie, Professor of Economics at the University of Chicago. The latter wished to have the assistance of a management expert and a trade unionist. For the management expert, he chose Robert G. Valentine.

Valentine was Commissioner of Indian Affairs in the Roosevelt Administration, and had later become "industrial counselor." We know Taylor's uncompromising position towards labor unions. Valentine, however, had a definite but quite different approach to the question of labor unions and "arraigned scientific management on the ground that it did not recognize the fact that unions are here to stay and that while they exercise the greatest power in behalf of the laboring people, scientific management is doing nothing to aid them in the work they

1. Commission on Industrial Relations; Final Report and Testimony. Congress 64, 1, Sen. Doc. No. 415, p. 1016.

are undertaking."[1] This would seem to indicate that no outspoken "Taylor-man" was taken as an expert. Valentine, however, was well acquainted with scientific management.

Having secured the assistance of Valentine, Hoxie appointed John P. Frey, Editor of the International Molders' Journal, of Cincinnati, as his trade union expert.

Preliminary to the investigation, Hoxie drew up a list of "Trade Union Objections to Scientific Management" and had it revised and approved by a committee of the American Federation of Labor. Similarly, he drew up a list of "Labor Claims of Scientific Managers."

Taylor, Gantt and Emerson were then requested to designate the shops to be investigated. Only these designated shops were visited by Hoxie and his assistants. They began their work early in January 1915 and it lasted, with occasional interruptions, to the end of April, 1915. A partial list of the plants and concerns visited is given below:

<u>Scientific Management Plants</u> (in whole or in part)

Tabor Manufacturing Company
The Link Belt Company
The Remington Typewriting Company
The H. H. Franklin Manufacturing Company, Syracuse, New York
The Standard Roller Bearing Company, Philadelphia, Pa.
Smith & Furbush Machine Company
Ferracute Machine Company, Bridgeton, New Jersey
Brighton Mills, Passaic, New Jersey
Acme Wire Company, New Haven, Connecticut
Sayles Bleacheries, Saylesville, Rhode Island
The Plimpton Press, Norwood, Massachusetts
The New England Butt Company, Providence, Rhode Island
The Watertown Arsenal
Jones and Laughlin Company, Pittsburgh, Pennsylvania

---

1. Bulletin of the Society to Promote the Science of Management, Vol. 1, December 1914, p. 3.

The Diamond Chain & Manufacturing Company, Indianapolis, Indiana
The Aluminum Casting Company, Detroit, Michigan
Joseph and Feiss, Clothcraft Shops, Cleveland, Ohio
The Black Company, Cleveland, Ohio
The Westinghouse Electric and Manufacturing Company, East Pittsburgh, Pa.
King Sewing Machine Company, Buffalo, New York
The Monarch Typewriter Company, Syracuse, New York
The German American Button Company, Rochester, New York
The Northway Motor & Manufacturing Company, Detroit, Michigan
Russell, Burdsall & Ward Bolt and Nut Company, Port Chester, New York

Other Plants:

Geo. Oldham & Sons Company, Philadelphia, Pennsylvania
Newton Machine Company, Frankfort, Philadelphia
Filene's Specialty Store, Boston, Massachusetts
Jones and Lamson, Springfield, Vermont
Ford Automobile Works, Detroit, Michigan

Time Study and Systematizing Concerns:

Sanford E. Thompson, Time Study Expert, Newton Highlands, Massachusetts
Miner, Chipman and Staff, Cambridge, Massachusetts.[1]

Hoxie set up the following as "standards of judgment:"

"First, scientific management, in its relations to labor,
must be judged not merely by the theories and claims, either
of its representatives or opponents, but mainly by what it
proves to be in its actual operation. Mr. Taylor, especially,
has intimated that if any principle of scientific management
which he has laid down is violated, scientific management
ceases to exist. Evidently, the acceptance of this dictum
would lead to endless quibbling, and would prevent the drawing of significant conclusions as to the actual character and
tendencies of scientific management and its effects upon
labor welfare. It would be as true to say that the church
and the state rest upon certain fundamental principles, and
that if any of these are violated in practice, church and
state cease to exist ...

"Secondly, it follows that the scope of scientific
management -- what features are to be included under it --
is to be determined, again not by the theories of its
leaders, but by what is found to exist and persist in the system-
atized portions of shops designated to represent it ...

---

1. R. F. Hoxie, Scientific Management and Labor, pp. 3-4.

"Throughout the study here represented, therefore, scientific management must be understood to mean the system created and applied by Mr. Taylor, Mr. Gantt, and Mr. Emerson, and their adherents, as these systems actually work out in the shops designated by them, and to include whatever policies and methods investigation has proved to be characteristic of such shops, bearing in mind that the movement at present is not fixed and final, but is in its early stages of development."[1]

The investigation lasted three months and Hoxie's report is too long and detailed to present here. The conclusions he drew are quoted from his report:

"Scientific management, fully and properly applied, inevitably tends to the constant breakdown of the established crafts and craftmanship and the constant elimination of the skill in the sense of narrowing craft knowledge and workmanship except for the lower orders of workmen. Some scientific management employers have asserted belief in their ability to get on a paying basis within three months should they lose their whole working force except the managerial staff and enough others to maintain the organisation, if they had to begin all over again with green hands. What this means in increased competition of workmen with workmen can be imagined ...

"But beyond all this, time study strikes at the heart and core of the principles and conditions which make effective unionism and collective bargaining possible with respect to certain essential matters. When the employer can constantly initiate new methods and conditions and reclassify the work of the workmen, he can evade all efforts of the union to establish and maintain definite and continuous standards of work and pay. Time study is in definite opposition to uniformity and stable classification. It enables the employer constantly to lop off portions of the work from a certain class and then to create new classifications of workers with new conditions of work and pay ...

"Under these circumstances the progressive degeneration of craftmanship and the progressive degradation of skilled craftsmen seems inevitable ..."[2]

Some credit, however, was given to scientific management for its accomplishments in the last paragraphs as follows:

---

1. Hoxie, R. F., Scientific Management and Labor, p. 12.
2. Ibid, p. 16.

"Our industries should adopt all methods which replace inaccuracy with accurate knowledge and which systematically operate to eliminate economic waste. Scientific management at its best has succeeded in creating an organic whole of the several departments of any institution establishing a coordination of their functions which has previously been impossible, and, in this respect, it has conferred great benefits on industries.

"The social problem created by scientific management, however, does not lie in this field. As regards its social consequences neither organized nor unorganized labor finds in scientific management any adequate protection to its standards of living, any progressive means for industrial education, any opportunity for industrial democracy by which labor may create for itself a progressively efficient share in management. Therefore, as unorganized labor is totally unequipped to work for these human rights, it becomes doubly the duty of organized labor to work unceasingly and unswervingly for them, and, if necessary, to combat an industrial development which not only does not contain conditions favorable to their growth, but, in many respects, is hostile soil."[1]

Taylor had been skeptical on the outcome of Hoxie's investigation. In a letter to Henry P. Kendall in January 1915, he wrote that he had no hope that either Valentine or anyone else could convince labor that there was any good in scientific management. "I most sincerely hope," he wrote, "that some good will come out of Hoxie's investigation, but I do not believe it. At any rate, I feel that it is of the utmost importance to use every effort to make good come out of it, if possible."[2]

The strain under which Taylor had been working the past few years began to tell on him. There is no doubt that he sacrificed his health to the cause of scientific management. Before the Hoxie investigation was completed, he died of pneumonia on March 21, 1915.

General Crozier paid this tribute to Taylor soon after his death, in the closing words of an address he delivered before the Philadelphia School of Commerce and Accounts:

1. R. F. Hoxie, Scientific Management and Labor, p. 141.
2. Copley, Vol. 2, p. 246.

"It has been more than once represented to me that I have increased the difficulty of maintaining scientific management in the Ordnance Department by calling it the 'Taylor System,' and that I would have less difficulty if I should suppress this name, which is declared to be anathema to organized labor. I have not cared to do this. I regard Mr. Taylor as the father of scientific management, without intending to detract from the credit of its able apostles. We have employed Mr. Taylor's system, installed with the aid of an expert designated by him, and in its actual practice we have had a fair measure of the success which he promised. We hope we are not through with improvement and with the attainment of further success. I believe that the credit which is due to the founder of the system should be rendered by using his name in connection with the employment of it, and I am unwilling to render the task of employing scientific management in the arsenals of the Ordnance Department more easy of accomplishment through disassociation from it of the name of the great man to whom it is due."[1]

The Significance of the Period 1900-1911.

Although this period covers but a single decade of time, it is of considerable significance in the development of scientific management. This is true not because this period was characterized by numerous events of significance but rather because discussion, analysis, argument, and exploration concerning ideas, philosophies, and practices in the field of management were carried on in many places in an extensive manner. Reference was made in Chapter III to the formation of the A. S. M. E. and the A. F. of L., both of which organizations functioned as media for the dissemination of ideas and theories during this period, and at the same time brought together opposing schools of thought for a discussion and deliberation. During this period, also, many so-called corporation schools were formed by large enterprises. It is reasonable to interpret this move as a recognition of the fact that employees needed to be better trained in order to learn and practice the new methods and

---

1. Copley, Vol. 2, p. 352.

to operate under the changing management policies which were beginning now to be applied with reference to labor and various other phases of shop management.

We also note during this period the formation of the School of Commerce, Accounts, and Finance of New York University, which is a further recognition of the rising need for training of individuals in the fundamentals of business operation. Clearly the growth of transport and communications facilities were also of great significance in disseminating information concerning management during this period and of stimulating the exchange of ideas and points of view with respect to the theories and practices put forward. Many capable men joined with Frederick Taylor during this period to advance his ideas and theories of shop management and to give wider publicity to them through the presentation of papers before groups of business men and through the application of Taylor's methods in business establishments. Outstanding among this group of men were Henry L. Gantt, Henry R. Towne, Frank B. Gilbreth, Henry S. Dennison, Carl Barth, Morris L. Cooke, Sanford E. Thompson and many others.

In 1903, Mr. Taylor published what is now considered a classic in the literature of management, "Shop Management." The publication of this book gave considerable impetus to the interest in and discussion of management, not alone from the viewpoint of the manufacturing plant but from the broader business point of view as well. The next publication of significance in this field was Harrington Emerson's "Efficiency" published in 1909. This was followed the next year with the publication by Henry L. Gantt of his book "Work, Wages, and Profits." The threads which have since woven themselves in the pattern we call scientific

management were now beginning to be brought together through the
development of a body of literature. It will be observed in Chapter V
that this movement gained considerable headway immediately following
the close of this period which has persisted up to the present time.
From the viewpoint of the dissemination through public utterances
and general publicity media of matters relating to management, the
widespread editorial and forum discussion of the Eastern Railway
Rate Case in 1910-11 is an outstanding example. From the private
letters and other data of these leaders, one readily finds evidence
to indicate that in the rapidly strengthening ranks of organised
labor, as well as among legislative and other official bodies, this
new subject of management was receiving considerable attention. There
was no unanimity of agreement as to what the principles of management
were, the extent to which they could be applied in any industry, the kinds
of industry in which they might be suitably applied or the values that
might arise from their application. In fact, opposition to the application of these theories and practices was already beginning to develop in
a rather pronounced fashion among labor groups. To those who had strong
convictions with respect to the need for and value of the new management,
these subversive movements brought sharply to their attention the need
for the formation of agencies through which full and free discussion
might be effected in order that those who were fearful of its social
and industrial consequences might have a better opportunity to fully
understand its purposes, methods, and outcomes. They realized also
that if the movement were to endure it was necessary to enlist a much
larger group of people in the cause and thus the need for more agencies
through which information could be disseminated was again emphasised.

The culmination of the interest and discussion during this period
was two events of tremendous significance in the management movement.

The first of these was the publication in 1911 by Frederick W. Taylor of his now famous classic book "Principles of Scientific Management." This may well be the landmark from which we can date the rise of scientific management in America. It was the first treatise on scientific management to be offered by any writer and it so clearly and convincingly expounded Taylor's philosophy and principles that it crystalized the thinking and convictions of a great many people with respect to the desirability of scientific management. During the same year a conference was held at the Amos Tuck School of Dartmough College on Scientific Management. This conference was under the leadership of Harlow S. Person, one of the pioneers in the scientific management movement. It brought together some three hundred business men, engineers, and statesmen representative of the entire country who gathered there voluntarily to listen to notable addresses by such men as Taylor, Gantt, and other outstanding leaders in the management movement. The discussions during this conference dealt not only with the philosophy and principles of management but with the varied problems of their application in all types of American enterprise. The conference not only helped to firmly establish the validity and acceptance of Taylor's principles, but it stimulated such a tremendous growth of interest in the management movement that the next few years saw a series of developments which placed the movement on a permanent and institutionalised basis. The following chapter will attempt to identify and to bring out the significance of these developments.

The practical value of these principles and laws in the operation of an enterprise is not the issue here. They are cited because their development represents a step which appears to be identical with that followed in the development of most of the other sciences. Moreover, the critical analysis and evaluation of these principles in terms of their economic, political, and social importance suggests the idea that the responsibility for their application to situations which affect so profoundly all aspects of our economy should rest only in the hands of those individuals who have proven their qualifications for the task and who are willing to hold themselves accountable to society at large for the trust placed in their keeping. They are emphasised in this paper, therefore, because they represent a phase in the total development which is being analysed in an effort to determine if there is or is not any valid evidence to prove that management is moving toward professional status.

CHAPTER V

MANAGEMENT APPROACHING THE PROFESSIONAL STATUS

The Growth and Significance of Professional Associations

The leaders in the management movement, who had been instrumental in the formation and operation of the American Society of Mechanical Engineers, were well aware of the importance of this professional association in connection with the management movement. It was pointed out in Chapter IV that the need for additional agencies to sponsor and assist in the development and dissemination of management principles and practices was now recognized by these leaders as being very acute. It was therefore decided that action in this direction needed to be taken at this time while the interest in the subject was at high pitch and the enthusiasm for its development could be crystallized.

"The year 1912 marked the launching of an association for organized discussion of Taylor's doctrines and technique of scientific management which provided a definite impetus to the movement of scientific management. The Society to Promote the Science of Management was formed by a group of men devoted to the cause of practical development of the scientific approach to managerial problems. In 1915, the year of the untimely death of Taylor, the association was renamed the 'Taylor Society' in honor of the great leader. Continuing under this designation until 1934, an amalgamation of the Taylor Society and the Society of Industrial Engineers caused a revision of the title nearly to the original phrasing, namely, The Society for the Advancement of Management.

"In the year of the founding of the society, 1912, the Efficiency Society was organized in New York City but was of comparatively short life because of the limited scope of its outlook and program.

"Next was the Society of Industrial Engineers, organized in 1917 and designed, at the start, to supplement the work of the Taylor Society with more emphasis on production methods.

"In 1919 the National Office Management Association was formed, and in the same year the National Association of Cost Accountants.

"The Management Division of The American Society of Mechanical Engineers was next created in 1921.

"In 1922 the American Management Association was formed as a combination of earlier groups devoted to school and corporation training and to personnel. Later the scope of the Association was broadened to embrace all branches of management.

"A professional association of practicing management engineers was organized in 1929 under the designation of Association of Management Engineers.

"The American Marketing Society was founded in 1931. A number of local groups and organizations have been formed in various parts of the country. Several organizations have been formed in other nations.

"With the growth of these various societies working along different and sometimes parallel lines, it was decided in 1933 by a group of men influential in the different organizations that the time was ripe for the formation of a council of the various societies under the name of the American Management Council.

"Of vast international importance in the development of scientific management was the institution of the International Management Congress in 1923. This was initiated by the scientist-president, Masaryk, of Czechoslovakia, with the advice of American engineers. The congress met in Prague in 1924 and has been followed by congresses in Brussels in 1925; in Rome in 1927; in Paris in 1929; in Amsterdam in 1932; in London in 1935; and in Washington, D. C., in 1938, as the Seventh International Management Congress.

"So far in this brief history, scientific management has been treated chiefly from the standpoint of the shop. For here was the initial development. It was not until about the close of the fourth period and the date of the death of Dr. Taylor in 1915 that the breadth of the scientific approach to management of business and social problems, as already envisioned by Taylor, began to be realized.

"Possibly the most important element in Taylor's contribution was the thorough demonstration he gave of the applicability of the inductive method to all industrial and business problems. The classic studies of tool feeds and speeds pointed the way to other studies in the business field. The broad result in the change-over in the psychology of a generation of businessmen from the 'practical' and 'empirical' to the more systematic application of experimental methods is a result which far surpasses the actual procedures developed by Taylor and his associates." [1]

---

1. "The History of Scientific Management in America", Mechanical Engineering Magazine, Vol. No. 61, (September 1939), p. 671.
   Prepared by American History Committee for the 1938 International Management Congress.

Table No. 1

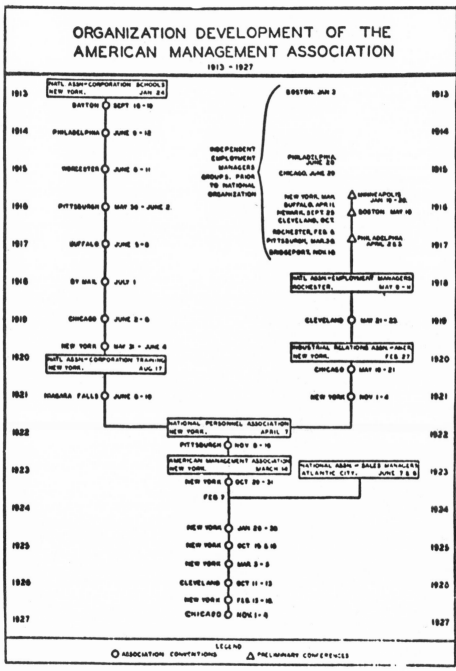

For the convenience of the reader and in order to show a little more clearly the chronological development of some of these professional associations, Table No. 1 is appended.

This does not comprise a complete list of the professional associations which are interested in one or another phase of modern management. Such agencies as the National Sales Executives Club, National Association of Purchasing Agents, Comptrollers Council of America, Retail Comptrollers Congress, Educational Buyers Association, American Economic Association, American Statistical Society, various accounting societies, and many others are active today in the discussion, development, and crystallization of management principles and practices.

There are no accurate yardsticks by which the influence of these associations upon the development of management can be measured. There is little doubt, however, as to their value. The fact that they are so numerous in number and that their membership is so large in total is conclusive evidence that business men are willing to pay money for the privilege of participating in the activities of these associations, in order that they may secure the many benefits available to them through such participation.

From the viewpoint of the further development of management, the value of these associations has been and is very great. They have done much not only to preserve and clarify the early literature and developments in the broad field but they are fostering many research projects and other undertakings which will have both immediate value to their members and future value to those who succeed the present generation. These associations have done much to emphasize the need for highly developed skills and abilities as well as a professional attitude on the part of those charged with managerial responsibilities. In fact, it has been largely through

the work of these professional bodies that various phases of management
has already risen to professional status. They have brought pressure to
bear upon those who were and are being trained for various management
fields to qualify according to agreed standards and they have also exercised
influence upon state legislatures and quasi-legislative bodies the practice
to license these people who would become practitioners. Typical illustra-
tions of this are the certification of a public accountant and the need for
a license for an industrial engineer.

The Development of the Literature of Scientific Management

The thought was expressed in discussing the contributions mentioned
in Chapters III and IV that the beginnings of scientific management in the
broader sense might be dated from the publication of Taylor's "Scientific
Management" in 1911. The belief behind this remark was that as L. P. Alford
says in his book on Industrial Management that " * * * the beginnings of
the art and science of industrial management are dated from the publication
of some professional article or book which expounded the philosophy, principles, or practice of the author."[1] This would indicate that the beginnings
of management in this country could be marked with the dates of the early
papers mentioned in previous chapters. Inasmuch as these papers covered
such a small portion of the total subject and did not fully expound the
authors' points of view and beliefs, common consent has accepted the significant dates as those marking the publication of books dealing with the field.
Mr. Alford as a result of his thirty or more years of interest and contact
with this subject suggests the following as the significant dates:

---

1. L. P. Alford, Principles of Industrial Management for Engineers, p. 61

Date	Author	Book Title
1903	Taylor	Shop Management
1906	Taylor	On the Art of Cutting Metals
1909	Emerson	Efficiency
1910	Gantt	Work, Wages, and Profits
1911	Emerson	Twelve Principles of Efficiency
1911	Gilbreth	Motion Study
1911	Taylor	Principles of Scientific Management
1916	Gantt	Industrial Leadership
1919	Gantt	Organizing for Work
1919	The Gilbreths	Applied Motion Study [1]

The significance of the literature brought forth by these early leaders is understood only when one understands the philosophy set forth by each of them. Again referring to Mr. Alford's work, he has crystallized in a few words the meat and implications of the philosophy of four of the greatest of these pioneers as follows:

"Frederick W. Taylor believed that the principal objective of management should be to secure 'maximum prosperity for the employer, coupled with the maximum prosperity for each employee.' By maximum prosperity he meant low production costs and large dividends for the employer, high wages for the employee, and a high general level of excellence for the industry. He maintained that these objectives could only be attained by the acceptance of a new philosophy of industrial management, that of the scientific method, in place of the philosophy then commonly held, which he characterized as the management of 'initiative and incentive.'

"Taylor formulated his philosophy in a set of three essentials or principles:

(1) the substitution of a science for the individual judgment of the workman;

(2) the scientific selection and development of the workman, after each man has been studied, taught, and trained, and one may say experimented with, instead of allowing the workman to select themselves and develop in a haphazard way; and

(3) the intimate cooperation of the management with the workmen, so that they together do the work in accordance with the scientific laws which have been developed, instead of leaving the solution of each problem in the hands of the individual workman.

"Henry Laurence Gantt, who had been associated with Taylor in much of the latter's early work, supported his chief's emphasis on the importance of science in industrial management, pointing out that the features that mark the new industrial spirit are: 'The substitution of the scientific method of determining what can be done as basis of action, instead of records of what has been done, or opinion of what can be done.' To this cold, scientific philosophy he added a humanizing

---

1. Ibid., p. 61

warmth: 'The era of force must give way to that of knowledge, and
the policy of the future will be to teach and to lead, to the advantage of all concerned.'

"As an ideal in industrial operation, Harrington Emerson directed
attention to the marvelous efficiency and lavish prodigality of
Nature. His philosophy he called the 'gospel of efficiency', and
stated it in this way:

'Efficiency does not consist in extreme effort, but
in the elimination of undesirable effort and waste of all
kinds, the elimination of child and woman labor in competitive employment. Efficiency does not come to increase the
nervous strain of the age, which gives railroad spine to the
locomotive engineer, and results in premature exhaustion of
the telephone girl, but it comes to palliate that strain by
standardizing both effort and reward....It comes todetermine
justly and without reference to wage rate, the standard time
of any operation, and to guarantee to each worker, whether
low or high, a special reward in proportion to individual efficiency.
'Efficiency means that the right thing is done in the
right manner, by the right men, at the right place, in the
right time.
'True efficiency means ameliorating conditions for the
worker, both individually and collectively—not only for the
worker, but also for the employer—not only for the employer,
but also for the corporation, and finally for the nation.'

"Frank B. Gilbreth declared that there is one best way to perform an operation or do a piece of work in industry. This teaching
may appear to be a doctrine of unattainable perfection. Rather,
it is a statement of the philosophy of the engineering standard.
The 'one best way', interpreted as an engineering concept, is the
best way that is known, or can be discovered, at any moment of consideration. It is not an ultimate best way but is in the line of
progress and may be changed or modified immediately a better way is
discovered. The new way then becomes the best way until it in turn
is superseded by something better than itself. To the one who ac-
cepts and applies this philosophy comes the grace and rhythm and perfection of motion of him who knows, and knows that he knows, and does
what he knows, no matter what is work may be." [1]

It is interesting to note in addition to the major works mentioned

in Mr. Alford's list that this period w a s p r o d u c t i v e

of considerably more literature relating to the field of general management

as well as to many of its specialized branches. Among other authors whose

---

1. Ibid, p. 61

contributions serve to amplify the fundamental ones already mentioned
and in many instances to advance new ideas or to expand the philosophies
or principles of these earlier writers may be mentioned A. Hamilton Church,
John William Schulze, Lee Galloway, Edward D. Jones, Dexter Kimball,
Oliver Sheldon, L. P. Alford, W. B. Cornell, Henry Dennison, J. B. Mooney
and Allan Riley, Rex Robinson, Ralph Davis, and many others. Each of these
writers, as well as many others not mentioned, has undertaken to present new
theories or interpretations of the principles or philosophies previously
stated, has made applications of these principles, or has attempted to re-
fine them to such an extent that they could be understood more readily and
applied more effectively.   It is interesting to observe in connection with
the works of the authors referred to that they have based their development
of principles largely upon the principles originally enunciated by Taylor,
Gantt, Emerson, and Gilbreth.

A more extended statement of principles was first set forth by
Henri Fayol in his "Industrial and General Administration" which was first
published in the form of a paper presented before a French technical society
in the fall of 1916. Mr. Fayol listed the following principles as the basis
for the development and application of the art and science of management
to industrial activity:

> "1. Division of labour.
> 2. Authority.
> 3. Discipline.
> 4. Unity of command.
> 5. Unity of management.
> 6. Subordination of individual interests to the common good.
> 7. Remuneration.
> 8. Centralisation.
> 9. The hierarchy.
> 10. Order.
> 11. Equity.
> 12. Stability of staff.
> 13. Initiative.
> 14. Esprit de Corps."[1]

---

1. Henri Fayol, Industrial and General Administration', p. 19

These principles constitute in large part the groundwork upon which the present body of laws and principles rest and to some extent the raw materials out of which new principles and laws have been formulated.

John William Schulze in his book "The American Office: its Organization, Management and Records" undertook to apply the principles set forth by the early leaders to the specialized field of office operations, while Dexter Kimball undertook to expand them somewhat and given them a broader application in the field of manufacturing. In 1923, Oliver Sheldon published his "The Philosophy of Management" which at the same time constitutes the foundation for these principles and an exposition of their philosophic implications. Shortly after this, L. P. Alford derived from these principles in part and from research and scientific analysis a series of laws to govern the management of manufacturing. A further elaboration of the principles and laws set forth by Taylor, Fayol, and Alford was made by W. B. Cornell in 1928 in his book "Industrial Organization and Management." Many other students of the subject have as a result of their labors and researches added to and assisted in the clarification and validation of these principles and laws.

It is generally conceded that the field has not been completely explored and a witness of this is L. P. Alford's latest book "Principles of Industrial Management for Engineers" published within recent weeks.

It is perhaps optimistic at this time to refer without some qualification to the science of management, although it is clearly evidenced by the references above quoted that the science of management is making rapid progress along many fronts. Such a conclusion carries with it many implications with respect to the questions raised in this thesis and it is believed that the additional evidence presented in this chapter, together with that presented in the preceding chapters, earmarks certain trends in the movement.

The World War period had a profound influence on scientific management. The War brought with it a greater demand for goods from the American market which, because of the scarcity of labor, could only be met by greater efficiency. Methods of greater efficiency and in some cases scientific management were introduced into plants in the United States. The formulation of principles among scientific management leaders, it was now found, had been incomplete. The Russian Revolution, as well as the program announced by the United States upon entering the War, were probably the most important factors in bringing a new philosophy with a wider conception of democracy into the system. The time of autocratic control of industry had definitely passed. This new spirit brought with it a mellowing in authority which in turn helped to make for more satisfactory relationship and greater harmony. In other words, while Taylor's revolution had been mostly in the mechanical field, "the mental revolution" became the all-important factor.

In 1919, Gantt was one of the leaders in a movement against industrial control by absentee stockholders and bankers and pointed to the shortcomings in our war production due to the fact that the industrial engineer was not given his proper place. Instead, the businessman with his "business for profit" motive was called to Washington to organize the war industries. When we read the chapter on "The Parting of the Ways" in Gantt's last publication, "Organizing For Work", we are surprised at what seems to us a rather radical attitude on the part of a leader in industry. He said, for instance:

> "The business man says profits are more important to
> him than the service he renders; that the wheels of busi-
> ness shall not turn, whether the community needs the ser-
> vice or not, unless he can have his measure of profit. He
> has forgotten that his business system had its foundation
> in service, and as far as the community is concerned has
> no reason for existence except the service it can render." [1]

---

1. Gantt, H. L., Organizing For Work, p. 5

He also predicted a deadlock between the business system and the community if a clash between these two ideals should arise. And since "laissez-faire" did not promise any solution of the problems, he said that we had come to a "parting of the ways", or else we would be drifting towards an economic catastrophe such as Europe exhibited at that time. In order to stave off disaster action should be taken quickly. In other articles which he wrote at that time (1919-1921) he gave warnings of an impending break-up of business and industry. Gantt had a deep insight into conditions of his day, and we must place his predictions alongside the events of the past years — the depression of 1920-1921, the boom years prior to 1929, and the depression which followed which was one of the most severe this country has ever experienced.

Gantt felt a great apprehension because business made profits which he deemed were beyond a just reward for the services it rendered, of which no good could come. He said:

> "We all realise that any reward or profit that business arbitrarily takes, over and above that to which it is justly entitled for service rendered, is just as much the exercise of autocratic power and a menace to the industrial peace of the world, as the autocratic military power of the Kaiser was a menace to international peace. This applies to Bolshevists as well as Bankers." [1]

Gantt drew attention to the fact that he was not suggesting something new, but simply going back to the first principles which were still in existence in rural communities, where the emphasis is placed on the "service" rather than on the "profit" motive.

Definite steps forward were made in coordinating individual leadership with group control. Valentine who had been one of Hoxie's advisors had already pointed out that "The days of compulsion — the days of service

---

1. Ibid., pp. 7-8

without consent — are over." [1]   Valentine divided the conception
of consent into two kinds or types, i. e., individual and group consent.
He had always taken the position that industry could be very efficient
and at the same time democratic. Cooke took the same position and carried
the idea further in his article "Who Is Boss In Your Shop." [2]   In this
paper Cooke noted the changes which had taken place in the labor movement,
many of whose leaders now admit that increased production is the only road
to a higher social and economic status. To him, scientific management stood,
"first, last and all the time for increased production." In regard to this
new attitude by scientific management towards labor he wrote:

> "It is not desirable to have a man do a thing merely
> because I tell him to do it. Obedience is rather a primitive
> virtue. I wish my associates to assume that I am sincere in
> wanting them to do only those things which they elect to do
> after as full an acquaintance with the facts as the conditions
> under which the work must be done makes possible. It very
> rarely occurs that things fail of the doing on account of this
> attitude. In other words, 'consent' may be interpreted as
> something larger than the opportunity to vote on each individual
> problem." [3]

Cooke believed "that the most important function of management is
to develop within the factory an educational system designed to get
every employee 'going from within so that he will run himself' in order
that he may gradually assume a larger and larger share in the general
conduct of the business." [4]   But there are few people in the labor rank
who want to assume any broad responsibility. "Hereafter the Captain,
whether of industry or of government, will necessarily be the man who

---

1. Robert C., Valentine, The Progressive Relation Between Efficiency and
        Consent, reprinted from the Bulletin of the Taylor Society in
        Hunt, E. E. "Scientific Management Since Taylor", p. 204
2. Morris Llewellyn Cooke, "Who Is Boss In Your Shop", Annals of the
        American Academy of Political & Social Sciences, Vol. 71, May 1917.
3. Ibid., p. 175
4. Ibid., p. 177 (He quotes this sentence from Drury)

loves, and loving, understands, and understanding, builds and leads and inspires great number of his fellows." [1]   But just having a union at a plant, or admitting one, does not necessarily mean cooperation. "Ninety-nine manufacturers out of one hundred who have unions have them only because they cannot help themselves." Again, a plant may be organized by labor simply because conditions are so satisfactory that the very fact that it was a non-union shop would be a constant reflection on the organized labor movement. What we actually need is a new technic for the individual and a new reference for him. All these problems call for leadership and the responsibility for this lies at the door of the leaders.

> "In the development of a true leadership lies the great hope of democracy — whether it be political or industrial. Only through enlightened leadership can we establish a proper relation of the group or mass to the individual, and the leader is he who points the way and pushes on and gaining one eminence uses it only as the basis from which to climb higher.

> "We can be reasonably sure that the leadership of the future will be far removed from the military ideal which has stood civilization in good stead to date." [2]

To be such leaders, men must first know their jobs. Then they must have ability, judgment, experience, enthusiasm and vision in the execution of their tasks. Nor can the leader of the future be hidden. He must visualize these facts and their capacity to his several constituencies.

> "It is not enough for the officer of a company or the superintendant of a shop to be honest, active and able. He must make his associates know this. He must keep his constituency convinced and with an ample factor of safety. If we are to have cooperation we must have genuine, relentless publicity affecting every relation.

---

1. Mourir Llewellyn Cooke, "Who Is Boss In Your Shop." Annals of the American Academy of Political & Social Sciences, Vol. 71, May 1917. pp. 181-182.
2. Ibid., pp. 181-182.

"The picture of a frock-coated and portly gentleman
sitting solitary and silent behind a roll-top desk in the
front office during those rare intervals between meetings
at the bank and at the board of trade is no longer our symbol
for industrial leadership. We demand more and more frequent
points of contact with our leaders, we prefer to be the president's associates rather than his men. The sphinx is increasingly at a disadvantage in comparison with the man who
can place his cards on the table. Whether it be for the
employer of five, or fifty, 5,000, or 50,000 makes little
difference — self-revealment, incessant and studied, but
above all true to the facts — has become the great moving
force. Science is beginning to illumine all the work of
men. Everywhere, even in the humbler tasks she provides an
art. Our industrial relations are no longer for the isolated
plant only. They are trade-wide, industry-wide, nation-wide,
yes, world-wide. Into this maze, if men would tread with free-
dom, love must enter. The dream will never come true through
collective bargaining alone." [1]

This is what Cooke called individualistic leadership. Under it,
it was the practice to no longer issue orders, which in turn will compel us to keep our man convinced. The result will be that the associates
carry out "what has become their own purpose as well as yours."

The charge which Gantt made against the business man's failure in
the organization of the work in Washington during the War was, however,
still another aspect. The chief executive's responsibility was the
organization of the enterprise. But as Kendall stated:

"I used to think that organizing ability and executive
ability were practically synonymous terms. I have changed
my opinion on that; and one of the most convincing experiences
which would have caused me to change my opinion, had I not
done so earlier, occurred in Washington during the war. Many
a big man, with the reputation of being in his business a
superman, came to Washington and failed signally as an organizer! In his own business he had been all his reputation
claimed as an executive working out policies and making
routine decisions day after day; and it was concluded, therefore, that he would be a great organizer; but when it came
to creating new organizations in Washington — that was quite
another matter! Why, Because the difference between organizing or creative capacity and executive ability was usually
not recognized when men were called to service in Washington." [2]

---

1. M. L. Cooke, "Who Is Boss In Your Shop." Annals of the American
Academy of Political & Social Sciences, Vol. 71, May 1917. p. 184.
2. Henry P. Kendall, "The Problem of the Chief Executive", in Hunt,
Scientific Management Since Taylor, p. 67. First printed in the
Bulletin of the Taylor Society, Vol. 7, No. 2, 1922.

When the United States entered the World War, Cooke offered his
services to the Government and became Chairman of the Storage Committee
of the War Industries Board. The period, in fact, was marked by a shift
of scientific management men from commercial work into government service.
A new form of stock control was developed by Gantt, Hathaway, Heckman,
Babcock and others. They did some work for the Supply Division of the
Ordnance Department and later similar work was done for the Supply
Division of the Quartermaster's Department. Although scientific management
in its more refined points could not be introduced in the different Government departments, where at one time or another scientific management men
were active, the general principles were nevertheless applied.

Beginning with the time of the outbreak of the World War more attention was paid to public opinion at the plant and to social life. This
was part of the movement towards greater democracy in our industry. This
movement found expression in the Clothcraft Shops of the Joseph and Feiss
Company and in the German American Button Company (Rochester, New York).

In 1917, Richard A. Feiss gave an address before the Convention of
the National Association of Clothiers on "The Spirit of Scientific Management." This address was later printed. In it Feiss said that some people
thought that scientific management was simply a system or a method by which
something could be done faster or cheaper, or that it was a wage system and
time study work.

> "It is not any or all of these. It is a science and a
> philosophy. Its purpose is not to speed up production, but
> to harmonize the relationship between management and men.
> There are no Aladdin-like results. There is no secret or
> hidden short-cut to achievement. It means more and harder
> work for the management. It puts everyone from the head of
> the concern down, and places the responsibility for accomplish-
> ment where it belongs." [1]

---

1. R. A. Feiss. Address on "The Spirit of Scientific Management."

We clearly see here how the emphasis was placed on harmonious relations. After the technical problems were solved and the mechanical improvements made, the human aspect involved and the betterment of the relationship between employer and employee had to be considered. There were no short-cuts, no Aladdin-like results. These words indicate a greater insight into the questions involved.

Comparing the old military type of management with the new conception, Feiss also said that the new order was "based upon responsibility and instruction," Scientific management could not begin at the bottom; it had to begin at the top. It must originate and "begin in the mind of the manager or the man in control. He must begin by broadening his vision." In the process of standardization of equipment nothing could be left to chance. In the standardization of equipment and materials, time and motion study make their first appearance. It assisted in establishing the best means and methods and all other conditions of operation.

Previous to the entrance of the United States into the World War, Gantt served as Consulting Engineer for the Frankford Arsenal. As we have already pointed out, after our entrance into the War he gave his full time to serve the government. His most noticeable achievements were:

"Controlling the production of rifles, guns, ammunition, and other war material for the army.

"Speeding the building of ships for the Emergency Fleet Corporation.

"Improving the operation of ships for the Shipping Board." [1]

In order to facilitate his efforts, he perfected the Gantt Chart as a managerial tool. He selected "rivets driven", as a unit of measurement of the progress in shipbuilding, and for the measurement of the performance

---

1. L. P. Alford, Henry Laurence Gantt, p. 192.

of ships he used the "ship hour." Gantt worked with several agencies of
the government. First, as already mentioned, he worked for the Ordnance
Bureau of the United States Army, then for the War Industries Board, the
Emergency Fleet Corporation, the Shipping Board, and finally in the production of naval air-craft. How Gantt got the opportunity to develop the
method of control of army ordnance material is best illustrated in the
following which is part of a letter General William Crozier sent to
Mr. Alford in 1920:

> "As soon as we got into the World War I realised that
> the immense expansion of production would soon place us in
> possession of a quantity of finished articles and partially
> worked materials, and in a position with reference to manu-
> facturing orders and deliveries, which would be utterly be-
> wildering unless we could establish a better system for keep-
> ing track of our output and supply than had ever been found
> necessary in time of peace. I therefore sent for Mr. Gantt
> and asked him to assume the task of installing in the De-
> partment a method which would keep us continually informed
> as to our state of progress, so that we might at all times
> know where we stood and what we had to expect. I wanted him
> to accept a commission in the Department, but he thought he
> could do better work as a civilian, because he also expected
> to work for the assistance of certain civil agencies of the
> Government in providing for the war, and I deferred to his
> opinion.
>
> "Mr. Gantt installed his system of straight-line charts
> for keeping track of production, and gave much assistance in
> securing personnel for handling them, some of whom were com-
> missioned and some employed, and I relied upon them greatly
> for my own information and that of my principal officers." [1]

To get data quickly on any particular subject and in order to have
the facts, General Crozier always went to Gantt. Gantt had one great
purpose in his war work; he wanted to get the facts, fix responsibility,
decrease idleness, and forward production. [2] In this work he met with
opposition and his revelation of facts and failures often brought about
obstacles in his work and made him many enemies. His task with the
Emergency Fleet Corporation and the Shipping Board was of greater import-

1. L. P. Alford, Henry Laurence Gantt. p. 194.
2. Ibid., p. 196.

ance for he began it at a time when Great Britain was in danger of starva-
tion and when the Germans were sinking more ships than were being produced.
In fact, in 1917, German submarines sank 6,618,623 tons of shipping, while
the world production of new ships was only 2,703,345 tons. In this connection it is very difficult to appraise Gantt's contribution in meeting
such an unprecedented emergency but he gave his full knowledge of industrial method to this tremendous task. Fabricated ships were planned and
developed for mass production. During 1918, the Emergency Fleet Corporation had built 533 ships having a total of 3,030,406 tons.

The first Gantt Chart in "Industrial Management" was published
February 1918. The Gantt charts were first applied in connection with the
government work but after the War he began to introduce this new type of
chart into the plants of his clients. Up to the time of his death the
following applications had received the most attention:

    To record the progress of work.
    To record machine operation.
    To record man performance.
    To show the work ahead of a department or plant. [1]

In 1922 Wallace Clark published a book on "The Gantt Chart" which
was later translated into French, Italian, Polish, Czechoslovakian, German,
Spanish, Russian and Japanese. Clark called the Gantt Chart "the most
notable contribution to the art of management in this generation", because
the chart represented facts in relation to time.

In 1916 a book appeared on "Fatigue Study" by Frank B. and Lillian M.
Gilbreth. It was the most up-to-date study of the subject at that time
and brought out an important phase of the labor problem. As if in direct
answer to Hoxie's criticism, the Gilbreths pointed to the scientific in-

---

1. L. P. Alford, Henry Laurence Gantt, p. 213.

vestigation on which fatigue study must rest. Fatigue study, in order
to be effective, requires special training of experts and the necessary
laboratory and equipment. Gilbreth also advised that colleges gather all
that had been done for the elimination of fatigue, starting a "fatigue
museum", and in this way that could "help in a second way by making
fatigue study a subject in the curriculum."[1]

In 1917 H. K. Hathaway presented a paper before the Taylor Society
on the "Maintenance of Machinery and Equipment as Part of the Taylor
System of Management."[2] In this paper, Hathaway pointed out the importance of systematic inspection both of machines and equipment, and
making the necessary repairs and replacements as part of scientific management. Improvements and changes in machinery, tools and other equipment
went hand in hand with time and motion studies to make the introduction
of the system a success.

In 1917 a paper was presented by Robert L. Dickinson, suggesting
the introduction of scientific management into hospital organizations.
The paper had first been presented and exhibited before the Harvard
Medical Club, but was declined by the leading hospital and surgical journals. In this paper on "Scientific Management and Hospital Organization",
Dickinson attempted to bring time and motion study to the attention of
the medical profession. A more positive contribution was made by
Arthur B. Green, who reported on a successful application of scientific
management methods in the art of paper making.

Of the advancements of scientific management abroad, mention should
be made of the increased application of scientific management principles
in plants which were under the direct control of the French Ministry of
War. In August 1917 a circular was sent out by the Ministry of War

1. Gilbreth, Frank B. and Lillian M., Fatigue Study, p. 153.
2. See Bulletin of the Taylor Society, Vol. 3, No. 3, May 1917, pp. 6-10.

signed by Clemenceau, in which instructions were given on "Industrial Methods." These instructions called for the creation of planning departments, asked managers to realize the problems created through the shortage of labor, and, therefore, it was expected that management and labor would cooperate, using the planning department as an intermediary.

In a similar circular dated February 26, 1918, and again signed by George Clemenceau, the French Ministry of War, pointed out that all heads of Military Establishments should turn to the study and application of methods of work fitting the exigencies of the moment, and recommended that the heads of plants and of their planning departments should study and consult various works in which the Taylor System was described. [1]

In 1920 Herbert Hoover, who at that time was Chairman of the European Relief Council, was elected the first president of the Federated American Engineering Societies. One of his first acts was to suggest an investigation and study into the restrictions and waste in industry. This marked the beginning of a movement in a new direction; the recognition of the fact that highest efficiency in industry can only be obtained after all industries are studied and improved as a whole.

In January 1921, Hoover appointed fifteen engineers who formed the Committee on Elimination of Waste in Industry. Later, two more members were added to this committee, so that the total membership now included the following men:

> J. Parke Channing, L. W. Wallace, L. P. Alford, George D. Babcock, William R. Basset, F. G. Boburn, Morris L. Cooke, Harrington Emerson, Ira N. Hollis, Herbert Hoover, Edward Eyre Hunt, C. E. Knoeppel, Robert Linton, Fred J. Miller, H.V.R. Scheel, Sanford E. Thompson, John H. Williams and Robert B. Wolf.

---

1. Copley, Vol.1, pp. xxi.

The report of this committee was printed in the same year.

On February 14, 1931, Herbert Hoover delivered an address before the Executive Board of the American Engineering Council, Federated American Engineering Societies, at Syracuse, New York. From this address we quote:

> "... there is no limit to consumption except the total capacity to produce, provided the surplus of productive power is constantly shifted to new articles from those that have reached the saturation point of demand. For instance, we have the productive capacity wasted today that would improve the housing conditions of our entire people to the level perhaps only fifty per cent of them enjoy -- and at the same time not entrench upon our established necessity. I am not suggesting that the forces of production can be shifted by imperial direction. The practical thing that can be done is to eliminate some of the wastes and misfits in our production, and depend upon the normal processes of business and human desires to absorb them." [1]

Hoover then told his audience that the largest area of waste could be found in the periods of slack production and unemployment, which are due to variations of the economic cycle.

The investigation as well as the recommendations made to industry were along lines of scientific management. The new element in the spirit of scientific management was probably best expressed in the following part of the foreword to this report, written by Mr. Hoover:

> "We have probably the highest ingenuity and efficiency in the operation of our industries of any nation. Yet our industrial machine is far from perfect. The waste of unemployment during depressions; from speculation and over-production in booms; from labor-turnover; from labor conflicts, from intermittent failure of transportation of supplies of fuel and power; from excessive seasonal operation; from lack of standardization; from loss in our processes and materials -- all combine to represent a huge deduction from the goods and services that we might all enjoy if we could do a better job of it." [2]

---

1. Herbert Hoover; Industrial Waste. Bulletin of the Taylor Society, Vol. 4, No. 2, April 1921, p. 78.
2. Committee on Elimination of Waste in Industry of the Federated American Engineering Societies,"Waste in Industry", McGraw-Hill Co. New York, 1921. p. ix.

The report pointed out that industrial waste was not only caused by failure to use the time and energy of men, but also from the failure to use the productive equipment available. The following table gives an indication of the extent of the investigation:

Branch of Industry	Number of Plants Investigated
Building Industry	73
Men's Ready-made Clothing Manufacturing	9
Boot and Shoe Manufacturing	8
Printing	6
Metal Trades	16
Textile Manufacturing	13

Since management has the greatest opportunity to eliminate waste, the greatest responsibility must also rest with it, but the responsibility of labor is by no means less important. To substantiate this fact, the committee estimated that management's responsibility for waste could be placed at more than 50 per cent; labor's responsibility at about 25 per cent, while the rest was due to outside contact and influences, which, however, was the least important factor.

Under the heading of "Lack of Cost Control" the following result of a survey of New York City printing plants was given:

"56 plants use standard cost system.
187 plants with no cost system but with a knowledge of all general costs.
741 plants with no cost system and incomplete knowledge of general costs.

The first two groups made money; the last two lost money in 1919." [1]

Faulty sales policies caused cancellation of orders and returns amounting from 3 to 14 per cent, and 5 and 11 per cent respectively. In 1920, cancellation reached 33 per cent and returns 18 per cent. [2]

Unemployment was also a great source of waste. The average clothing

---

1. Committee on Elimination of Waste in Industry of the Federated American Engineering Societies, "Waste in Industry", McGraw-Hill Co., New York, 1921, p. 13.
2. Ibid., p. 15.

worker was idle 31 per cent of his time; the average shoe-maker 35 per cent; the building trade workman 37 per cent, etc. Waste was enormous with regard to idle plants and equipment. Clothing factories were built 45 per cent larger than necessary; printing establishments were from 50 per cent to 150 per cent over-equipped; the shoe industry had a capacity of 1,750,000 pairs of shoes a day and produced little more than half that number. [1] Waste was also due to restricted production and loss from ill health and industrial accidents.

Management was given the following opportunities and responsibilities for the elimination of waste:

Improvement of Organisation and Executive Control
Production Control through
    Balancing Productive Capacity and Demand
    Development of Purchasing Schedules
    Elimination of Cancellation and Curtailments of Returns
    Correlation of Production Schedules with Sales Policies
    Inspection
    Maintenance
Uniform Cost Accounting
Method of Wage Payment (equitable and just)
Standardisation of Product—Materials—Equipment
Performance Standardisation
Personnel Relations
Prevention of Accidents
Research [2]

However, labor had its responsibility to cooperate in increasing production and in the standardisation of work; to change its rules in regard to restrictions on output; it was also responsible for improving the health of workers and preventing accidents and cooperate in improving industrial relations.

The committee then pointed in its report to the responsibilities of the owners and the general public. It drew special attention to the opportunities given to trade associations and made definite recommenda-

1. Committee on Elimination of Waste in Industry of the Federated American Engineering Societies, "Waste in Industry", McGraw-Hill Co., New York, 1921, p. 18.
2. Ibid., pp. 24-27.

tions for the formation of such associations in lines where they did not as yet exist, as, for example, the clothing industry and the printing machinery trade. Trade associations had to be formed in all industries lacking comprehensive organization.

An opportunity for assistance also lay with the Government. It should create a national information service which would supplement private agencies, giving data on current production, consumption and available stock of commodities. Another field of endeavor for the Government was providing a national statistical service on employment re uirements and conditions throughout the country. It should further accept a body of principles for the adjustments of labor disputes, a national policy regarding health, and a national program for industrial rehabilitation should be encouraged. The Government should also help in a nationwide program of industrial standardization and simplification. It can do this by (1) standardizing its own demand and (2) bringing about cooperation between the different industries through their respective trade associations.

Federal laws should be revised wherever they interfere with the stabilization of an industry. The reader will notice how many of the recommendations have become law or have otherwise been put into practice.

In a paper presented before the Society of Mechanical Engineers on "Ten Years Progress in Management", Alford listed the following points; although the order in which they are named is not significant, they are the most important steps of progress made since 1912:

"a. A greater appreciation of the human factor in industry.

"b. The growing recognition that employees should have a voice in the management as relating to those questions that directly affect them.

"c. The recognition of the strategic position of shop foremen
and the necessity of more carefully selecting and training
them.

"d. The increased recognition of the value of fundamental principles.

"e. The recognition of, and in a large degree the adoption of,
standard systems of cost accounting from the point of view of
timeliness, as a barometer rather than history, as an instrument of production rather than a matter of finance.

"f. A great development in mechanical equipment, combined with
improved plant layout and building plants to fit manufacturing
processes.

"g. A marked advance in sales policies.

"h. A marked advance in substituting the trained, competent engineer for the old-'cut-and-try' type of executive." [1]

The technique of accountancy is old, but scientific management had

a great influence on it.--first, the technique of record keeping or

the actual construction of forms and the establishment of methods, in

short, the routine procedure; then the establishment of principles accord-

ing to which operating data in money terms were classified and valued.

After this came the presentation of the data in such form that the execu-

tive was able to read it. And finally the analysis and interpretation

of the data. The last point which became of increasing importance under

scientific management had to do with the control and planning for future

operation on the basis of accounting data which had been collected.

In 1921, the Taylor Society held a symposium on "Stop Watch Time

Study; An Indictment and Defense" which was led by Gilbreth. This

symposium was on the stop-w tch versus micro-motion study. Frank G.

Gilbreth and his wife led the attack on the stop-watch. According to them,

the use of the stop-watch resulted in inaccurate observation, hence, the

1. L. P. Alford, "Ten Years Progress in Management"; Proceedings A. S. M. E.,
1922, p. 1247.

final averages were no more accurate than the data from which they were derived. [1]

The methods used by Taylor were the best available at that time, but since then the attitude of the worker as well as of the general public has changed. Attention was also called to the increased knowledge which had been acquired in psychology, especially on the laws and phenomena of behavior, of habit formation, the phenomena of automacity and the learning process, all of which had advanced tremendously since the days of Taylor.

While micro-motion studies give consideration to the quality of the man, the stop-watch does not do so. In the discussion which followed, Carl G. Barth, Dwight V. Merrick and others took up the defense for the stop-watch method of making time studies. Barth based his defense on the difference between means and method by saying:

> "To my mind it is not so much the Means as the Method of using these that determines scientific as against un-scientific procedure." [2]

In 1923, a new factory building of the Jackson Mills, Nashua Manufacturing Company, Nashua, New Hampshire, was first planned and built in such a way as to insure a continuous flow of material from process to process. Humidifiers were installed, while a system of conveyers handled the entire product from raw cotton to finished cloth, moving it from one department to another with a marked savings in cost. The planning for each department was done in such a way that unnecessary waiting for material would be eliminated and provisions were made so as to always keep a minimum quantity in process. Careful analysis of what the looms

---

1. Frank L. & Lillian M. Gilbreth., Stop Watch Time Study: An Indictment and Defense; Bulletin of the Taylor Society, Vol. 3, June 1921, p. 100.
2. Ibid., p. 109.

really required resulted in a prepared schedule for work. [1]

Proper routing has become of increasing importance under scientific management and in some cases the question of success or failure depended to a great extent on routing. Management may be seriously handicapped in the application of scientific management principles where quantities were small and the operations short. In such cases refuge has been taken to what may be called "combination routing." Under this method, two or more batches which otherwise were handled separately during long operations were conveniently combined for shorter operations. The method was applied by Herrmann Aukman and Company at Lebanon, Pennsylvania, manufacturers of plain and embroidered handkerchiefs. [2] It required handling facilities and regular planning for the proper combinations.

Office Management.

The Curtis Publishing Company began in 1917 to standardize work in the office. Past records were studied, then special time and idle time, after which regular time studies were made on which the standards could be based. Office clerks worked on salaries, but penalties were set for errors and incentives for good production. To those who did not come up to standards, "extras" of one dollar or more per week were offered for the improvements they made. They received these "extras" up to the time they came up to standards, and from that time on bonuses were paid. [3] These ideas came in part as a result of success of incentive plans in the shop.

---

1. Norman T. Thomas, Significant Savings in Textile Mill Operation: Bulletin of the Taylor Society, Vol. II, No. 4, August 1924.
2. D. J. Walsh, Jr., "Combination Routing", Bulletin, Vol. 7, No. 4, 1924.
3. Walter B. Fuller, "Application of Scientific Principles to Office Management." Bulletin, Vol. IV, No. 3 (1919).

In about 1922, a Bureau of Methods was established as a separate department at the General Electric Company. The head of this new bureau had to report to the comptroller of the company. The duties assigned to this department were:

"1. Studies of office organization including the assignment of duties, selection and grading of clerical personnel...

"2. Making surveys of clerical problems, assisting in formulating standard practices and approving methods;

"3. Arranging physical layout of offices;

"4. Improving and standardizing wherever possible, reports rendered and forms used;

"5. Studies and recommendations looking to the largest possible use of mechanical labor-saving office appliances;

"6. Standardization of furniture and equipment;

"7. Organizing and installing stenographic transcribing; duplicators and other service bureaus;

"8. Preparation of office manuals." [1]

The department was made a staff organization and had no direct responsibility for, or supervision over, the actual carrying on of the clerical work of the company. Supervision was left in the hands of the responsible executive in each department. But the bureau acted as a coordinator and consultant; a clearing house for the broadcasting of new ideas, and as an originator of new routine.

In the same year (1922) Henry William Leffingwell presented a paper on "The Application of Principles of Scientific Management to the Office." [2] This paper was of special interest because it gave an opportunity to find along what lines scientific management had been developed in its application to the office in general.

---

1. H. V. Browne, Recent Office Economics, Office Management Series (1932).
2. Bulletin of the Taylor Society, Vol. VII, No. 1, February 1922.

Leffingwell thought that the analytical approach to any office problem was precisely the same as it would be in a factory. The first step in the introduction of scientific management into an office was to gain records of accomplishments which would give a basis for control. Control in turn must be based on some controlling unit such as orders or transactions. In the introduction of scientific management into a factory office, the order was made the controlling unit. While setting up standards, a study was made of everything that had to be filed. It was found necessary to determine a standard practice instruction, advising the filing clerk what should and what should not be filed. The result was that filing was reduced by approximately 25 per cent, with a corresponding reduction in space, equipment and filing energy. [1]

In the case of a department store, according to Leffingwell, a most complete set of executive control reports were prepared by the department head himself. In the merchandising department, control was perfected by setting quotas for each buyer and graphs were introduced showing, daily, the relative standing of each buyer. Similar charts were prepared for the bookkeeping department, showing when the statement clerk and bookkeeper had finished the work scheduled for them. For comparative purposes, photostats were made for the same day of each month and a constant improvement could be seen through this control. A rating plan was also established and then used to determine the base rates and to serve as a guide for possible promotions. A Personnel Division which had been organized had responsibility over the Employment, Training, Rating, Statistical, Timekeeping, Employees Restaurant, Hospital and House Organ Departments. [2]

---

1. H. W. Leffingwell, The Application of Principles of Scientific Management to the Office"/ Bulletin, Vol. VII, No. 1 (1922), p. 10.
2. Ibid., pp. 6-7.

Time records were also set up, bringing about a saving in time-keeping costs of 25 per cent in addition to furnishing a payroll which could be properly checked and credited. Rates reduced from 10 per cent to .5 per cent through the setting up of records on absences and tardiness; while errors were reduced .7 per cent through an analysis and search for causes. [1] Standardization was extended to the account books and in the case of the accounts payable book it was found that two-thirds of each sheet was left blank. By redesigning the books, waste space was eliminated through which the weight of the books was reduced by 62 per cent and the size by 44 per cent. Further savings were affected by consolidating several clerical departments in one large room and by introducing clerical tables of special design in place of desks. Standardization of mail-opening increased the output from 100 to 240 letters per hour. [2]

Leffingwell pointed out that little of this had been done in banks. The changes which were made were mostly of a physical nature, such as the standardization of equipment. The teller's equipment was standardized so that whenever the teller moved, rebuilding became unnecessary. Tables were standardized and made adjustable as to height. Special devices were fitted to the cages through which messages could be handed into the cage without the messenger entering it, nor could a hand be inserted. [3]

In 1923, the firm of Leffingwell-Ream and Company put into effect an Examination and Rating Plan "the purpose of which is to evaluate justly, dispassionately and as accurately as possible the management of an office."[4]

---

1. H. W. Leffingwell, The Application of Principles of Scientific Management to the Office; Bulletin, Vol. VII, No. 1 (1922), p. 8
2. Ibid. p. 10.
3. Ibid., p. 13
4. Bulletin Vol. X, No. 2, April 1925, W. H. Leffingwell, "The Present State of the Art of Office Management", pp. 99-104.

Under this plan the subject of office management was divided into 15 main divisions and 93 subdivisions. Each subdivision was rated separately and then ratings were built up for each division and the office as a whole. One of the divisions, in fact the one which received highest ratings was "Use of Office Machinery"; its average rating was 96 per cent. The next highest rating was received by "Intercommunications" with 83 per cent. Subdivisions of the latter were Telephone Service, Clerks at Desk, Messenger System and Necessary Mechanical Devices.

Problems in management seem to be affected by the period, i. e., the business cycle. Thus in 1932-1933, office managers were faced with conditions which called for immediate solution. It was termed a question of preserving the "human inventory." Industries and business came to the recognition that this was the most valuable asset and yet there was a combination of circumstances making for rapid depreciation.

These circumstances were mainly caused by the depression. On this, F. L. Rowland said: "The office worker who is subject to worry, debt, family financial difficulty, fear of unemployment, is deteriorating as surely as perishable goods exposed to the elements."[1] In coping with the situation the office manager will, no doubt, forget his own worries; it is a situation which calls for real leadership. It was found to be much better to tell the staff how long they may expect employment to last. The cutting of salaries which was so prevalent among business would have its limitation if executive and personnel morale were to be maintained.

Standardization.

Since the days of Taylor, standardization has had increased attention.

---

1. F. L. Rowland, "Present Status and Probably Future Trend in Office Management", American Management Association. Office Managers Series No. 61 (1933), p. 4.

Under organised efforts at promulgation we should mention: (1). Standard terms, (2) The functions and executive titles of a standard organisation, (3) Policy on bonus, (4) List of books for reference in industrial management. [1]

In regard to bonus payments the following factors call for standard definitions: Time allowance, money payment, rate base, earnings, etc. Also a standard bibliography of works on industrial management to be published by the Taylor Society.

While the promulgation of standard terms and clear definitions for such terms is of immense help as a tool in the work of standardisation, it is however only secondary in importance when compared with the ultimate object, which is the standardisation of the product itself. To effect economy on a national scale and a real elimination of waste, standardisation is the solution.

Copeland mentioned seven specific trade economies which could be obtained by standardisation. They are:

"1. Decrease in capital investment in all branches of the trade and in all individual plants.

2. Elimination of waste in experimentation and designing since designing in individual plants is unnecessary when scientific investigations and tests have been made by the trade.

3. More speedy and reliable delivery; the manufacturer being able to carry standardised stock for quick delivery.

4. It tends to decrease prices. (General decrease.)

5. The introduction of new machinery is facilitated and in many lines made possible.

---

1. Wm. O. Lichtiner, of Thompson & Lichtiner, Boston: "Promulgation of Standards by the Taylor Society", Bulletin Vol. 5, No. 5, August 1920, pp. 140-152.

6. It eliminates false and wasteful ideas prevalent in
the trade, relative especially to design,quality and
method.

7. Decrease of ruinous competition due to ignorance. It
means more dependable advance estimates of quality,
cost and time delivery."

On May 26, 1923, Herbert Hoover gave an address at the Department
of Commerce at Washington before the Conference of State Purchasing
Agents on the subject of "Industrial Standardization." In this address
he drew attention to the importance of standardization to the factor
of the elimination of waste. It insures quantity production and hence
lower cost, smaller investment of capital and, therefore, the release of
capital for other industrial purposes and developments. [1] Federal standards and tests have helped in many industries. In the case of the
cement industry practically the whole output of the country was produced
and distributed on the basis of federal standards and tests. If a pur-
chaser stated "federal specification", he would be sure to get the quality
he desired. It has made for uniformity and has improved the quality of
the products and has thus been a boon to the cement industry and even
more so to the construction industries. The work on commercial standards
and specifications has gone so far that many industries are applying to
the Department of Commerce to establish standards ··n which specifications
may be used.

The Division of Simplified Practice, Bureau of Standards of the
Commerce Department has as its object a reduction in the variety of
forms, sizes, etc. of the product of an industry through the voluntary
agreement of those in the industry. By 1924 more than 70 groups were
using the Division's service in working out definite simplified practice

---

1. E. E. Hunt, Scientific Management Since Taylor, p. 189.

recommendations. These agreements were usually made between manufacturers
and distributors. Here are a few results of such agreements: The variety
of vitrified paving bricks was reduced from 66 to 5; of bed springs and
mattresses from 78 to 4; and of milk bottles from 49 to 9. [1] While the
Division had no authority to compel such reduction,it could, nevertheless,
make surveys of existing diversities, sizes, varieties, finishes, brands,
and their relative importance, and through the results of such surveys,
manufacturers were usually anxious to make agreements with distributors
in order to secure the savings derived from standardisation and simplification. For the purpose of facilitating such agreements, the Bureau helped
in the arrangement of conferences of trade bodies and supplied them with
the forms in which such plans were set up.

Standards based on the best that is available and on accurate
measurements embodying the best practice known were called super-standards
by Gilbreth. By setting up such standards, Gilbreth did not mean that
they could never be improved upon, but they were recognised "as the
embodiment of the One Best Way extant and a further step towards the discovery of the One Best Way available at that time." [2]

Production and Sales Management.

At the close of the War, the adjustment to peace-time production
was one of the foremost tasks of industrial management. The Winchester
Repeating Arms Company reduced its force within a very short time from
20,000 to about 7,000 employees (1918-1919). It also began the manufacture

---

1. Bulletin Vol. IX, No. 5, October 1924. How the "Division of Simplified
   Practice Conferences with Organized Trade Bodies", By C. L. Barnum.
2. Frank B. & Lillian M. Gilbreth, "Super-Standards"; Bulletin Vol. VII,
   No. 3, June 1922, p. 110.

of other products than arms by entering the hardware field. One of its
new lines was the manufacture of pocket knives. Prior to the War one of
the largest manufacturers of pocket knives in this country made over six
thousand different patterns. The Winchester Repeating Arms Company, however,
thought that they would cover the need of their customers sufficiently
with a selection of 129 patterns. One might think that competition
would harm these efforts by offering greater diversity in pattern.
This was not true, in fact, this company was soon followed by the largest hardware jobber in the country who cut his line to 116 patterns.
These efforts were for standardization of products, but its effect on production and sales was twofold: first, it increased the size of the order
which could be placed in a factory in one lot; secondly, it meant a larger
turnover and smaller investment for the dealer who carried the goods. [1]

The manufacturing engineers were furnished with specifications for
packing methods, and samples were given from competitors' products. Efforts were made to put on all products the symbol number by which they
were designated on the factory orders and the accounting forms. The manufacturing engineers were also furnished with information of the peak-load
periods.

In 1919, in its efforts towards coordinating sales with production,
the Elliot-Fisher Company of Harrisburgh, Pennsylvania, looked up the
number of manufacturers rated between $5,000 and $10,000. It maintained a
record of the number of adding machines sold to this group. The money
value of sales to this group was divided by the number of manufacturers
of that size in the United States and this gave the company the "value

---

1. W. E. Freeland, Coordination of Sales with Scientific Production;
   Bulletin, Vol, 5, No. 5, October 1920, p. 205.

in the past per manufacturer thus rated." The same procedure was used
in order to arrive at the exact figure for the groups of larger and
smaller manufacturers. The knowledge obtained for each classification
was then reduced to individual territories and by this the company knew
the potential value of a manufacturer of a given size for the coming
year. [1] For the cities, the company used the block system in its
efforts to get the amount of potential sales. By a block, the company
meant "a county within a city." Once those to whom the products had been
sold within a given block were known and properly rated, firms were also
able to count possible prospects that have not been sold and rate them by
twelve business and four rating groups as the firm did with those to whom
it had sold its products in the past. In these attempts at coordinating
sales with production by finding the potential sales for the different
territories and blocks, the company had to make adjustments for the different groups of population.

The Sales Executive Conference, composed of the General Sales Manager
and Branch Managers, held on June 25, 1920, passed a resolution to send
a questionnaire to manufacturing organizations represented at the conference and to others in order to secure data on current practice in the
organization for and the conduct of sales operations with reference particularly to the coordination of selling and production. The questions were
on sales administration, sales engineering or planning, sales operating
and on general business subjects. [2]

In 1920, a report was presented before the Taylor Society on the
"Organization and Functions of the Sales Engineering Department." This

---

1. W. E. Freeland, Coordination of Sales with Scientific Production,
   p. 225.
2. Bulletin, Vol. V, No. 5, November 1920, pp. 231-234.

report was signed by Willard E. Freeland, of the Winchester Repeating
Arms Company, as chairman, by C. H. Keer of the E. J. du Pont de Nemours
Company, Henry T. Noyes of the Art in Button Company, and others. [1]

This report stated that the Sales Engineering Function presented at
least three distinct phases: (a) Field research, (b) Technical assistance,
and (c) Master planning and scheduling. It also pointed out that it should
be recognized that the major function of sales engineering was to analyze,
plan and schedule future projects, while the planning and scheduling of
current projects was a function of the operating division. "Sales engineering should become the coordinating function of the entire business." By
this it can relieve administrative and managerial executives of many of
their most troublesome and time-consuming problems. If sales engineering is months ahead of the operating departments, as.it actually should
be, then adequate time should be given to the purchasing, financial, personnel and production departments to plan for their respective activities.

The Dennison Manufacturing Company made a variety of about 10,000
items, from shoe tags to shipping tags in several colors, baggage checks
used by the railroads, marking tags of various kinds, gummed labels and
similar products. This great variety permitted the company to make possibly more than the ordinary amount of experimenting through which it could
in turn be of assistance to other companies. The company had a definite
sales policy which it consistently followed. Expansion of a certain
percentage was planned for each year. To bolster sales in times of depression new items were launched and a reservoir of ideas was kept to be
used in such times when sales resistance was usually greater. In addition

---

1. Bulletin, Vol. V, No. 6, December 1920, pp. 236-237.

to developing new merchandise for such periods, salesmen were specially trained in anticipation of a depression and with this augmented and well-trained sales force, the company was in a position to go through such years with a rate of operation which was little below normal. For its sales and production schedules, the company used a "master budget." Men of the selling organisation were directly in charge of the factory production. Production was reviewed monthly. Schedule sheets were made out which gave the sales of the previous year together with the estimates for the current year, plus the actual monthly sales of the current year and the total for same. The same schedule showed actual production per month and total production for the current year. On other sheets the sales over a long period of years were given and used for comparative purposes. This afforded a good view of the trend of the individual items.

The merchandise managers were in close touch with sales so that variations were discovered before the company ran out of stock or piled up too much of any one item. Next the company set production and sales quotas on the different lines of merchandise it was producing. In addition to the monthly schedule sheets, the company had yearly estimates. The sales quota for each important group of items was in accord with a long range program of increasing sales. Certain items have decided selling peaks during the year, hence the company developed its stock line so that it would balance the flood of orders coming for certain items all at once. A special graph was made for this purpose and during the dull months of the year, the company made boxes for its own goods in which its merchandise was sold to dealers and consumers. The "Master Budget of Sales and Production" [1] of this company was an excellent example of how

----

1. Bulletin, Vol. 7, No. 6, December 1922, see also Hunt, pp. 132-140.

scientific management principles could be applied to both production
and selling.

In some large establishments having many selling units it had become the practice to base the percentage of total overhead not on sales
but on the sales valuation of the territory which the selling unit or branch
covered. The Burroughs Adding Machine Company installed this system in
1904 and developed it continuously by analyzing the different territories
and digging up facts on which to base these quotas. [1]

The period marked the establishment of specialized research departments for the marketing and sale of their products by larger enterprises,
such as General Electric, American Telephone and Telegraph, etc. These
departments increa ed gradually in number and showed how business realized
to an increasing degree "that accurate information and competent analysis
are invaluable in the control of a business." [2]

Due to research and technical improvements, other firms similar to
the Dennison Manufacturing Company were able to bring production and sales
into a better relationship, or what is of even greater importance, to
regularize production where the demand for the product, or the supply,
was distinctly seasonal. The Hills Brother Company was the largest packer
and distributor of dates ("Dromedary") in the country. The peak for the
sale of dates was always during three months in the fall of each year.
Production followed demand. In order to distribute production more evenly
over the whole year, the firm tried first to stimulate a more even demand
by adjusting selling and advertising to serve this purpose. Then various
production methods were studied. In 1921, the company found a solution

1. Charles P. Staubach, Apportioning Sales Overhead; Bulletin, Vol. VII,
   No. 1, February 1922, pp. 27-33.
2. C. S. Yoakum, Present Status of Management Research Methods; Proceedings
   of the Institute of Management, Series No. 4, p. 22.

to its problem. Through chemical tests the temperature at which dates
keep best and longest was determined. After that the working schedule
was so arranged as to conform to the newer methods of packing; a cold
storage plant had also been erected. The result was the company manufactured practically an even amount regularly throughout the year. [1]
The solution came more quickly than in the case of the Dennison Manufacturing Company where years of detailed experiments had to be made before regularization was achieved. In both cases one of the chief objects had been
regularization of production with a view of regularizing employment. This
object was achieved by both companies.

While in the two examples just mentioned the object had been to
balance sales and production and regularize employment, other attempts were
made at controlling the business cycle. One of the most noteworthy attempts in this direction was made by the Walworth Manufacturing Company.
The first experiments showed that a Walworth cycle did exist. Through
records available in the treasurer's office a curve representing this
cycle could be worked back as far as 1890. Among the many letters coming
in from forecasting agencies giving advice on the cycle, it was found
that none of the services could be profitably used. But after studying
the Harvard Economic Service issued by the Harvard University Committee
on Economic Research, it was found that their forecasting was more definite and closer to the cycle of their own company than the forcasting
done by other agencies. Hence the company changed its curve to a form
which enabled a comparison with the Harvard B. curve. The war period
had to be omitted, but except for that, the curve could be plotted back

---

1. H. Feldman, *The New Emphasis in the Problem of Reducing Unemployment;*
   Bulletin, Vol. 7, No. 5, October 1922. See also Hunt, pp. 168-182.

to 1903 and was picked up again after the war, beginning with 1919. From 1921 on there was a faster rise in the Walworth curve than in the Harvard curve. When the rise began from the 1920-1921 depression, the company had the first opportunity of using the curve as a forecast to its activities; it used it in planning production based on the estimated sales. In addition to the control of production there were other adjustments which could be accomplished, such as monthly budget of sales, purchases, payroll and cash. On the results obtained Coonly stated:

"Here are the results for the year 1922; Our actual sales came within 0.5 per cent of our estimate. Cumulatively the first nine months were 4.3 per cent, but the full year's figures were so close to the estimate as to be a coincidence. We do not expect again to equal this particular record. We have reason to believe that the earlier months of the year were thrown out of line because of our increased ability to ship promptly. Having advance information, we were able to decide on a production plan that would give us an even flow of material throughout the year, building up our stocks in the spring and summer months to meet the fall demand. This accomplished not only better service to our customers, but greater economy of production, more even employment for our workmen and a great decrease in labor turnover. It enabled us to anticipate our material requirements and to take advantage of low price conditions. It gave our treasurer exact information as to financial requirements. It made it possible for me to place before our directors a definite estimate of the amount of money that would be involved in producing in advance the excess stock necessary for fall delivery, and it justified them in adopting the program because I could assure them that this investment could be liquidated before the end of the year. It enabled us to set up an ideal inventory for the end of the year and to work toward final liquidation to this ideal point. It proved that this inventory control was practicable, because we came within the limit set by my office." [1]

"Of all these benefits, probably the greatest has been our ability to operate on an even basis throughout the year." [2]

---

1. Howard Coonly, The Control of An Industry in the Business Cycle; Harvard Business Review, Vol. 1, No. 4, July 1923, reprinted in Hunt, E.E., Scientific Management Since Taylor, pp. 157-158. See also Barber, Joseph H. Coordination of Sales and Production at the Walworth Manufacturing Company. Bulletin, Vol. IX, No. 3, June 1924, pp. 112-131.
2. Ibid.

Master planning received increased attention. Under this form of planning a well-balanced and economically-directed business works out in advance a Master's Plan which in turn can be broken down into detailed schedules and budget for sales, finance and production.

It helped in the coordination between the different elements of a business and translated "market possibilities into a goal of production output. The steps in setting up a Master's Plan are given as follows: (1) Research, (2) Analysis, (3) Synthesis, (4) Planning, (5) Scheduling, (6) Inspection. Once we have a Master's Plan, we will have to determine the method of control." [1]

A Master's Plan has to be based on proper and skillful forecasting. Forecasting has become of increasing importance. In the cases of the Dennison Manufacturing Company, the Walworth Company and others, and their attempts at coordination of sales and production and the regularizing of employment, scientific forecasting plays an important role. Another example of attempts made in the same direction is that of the firm of Henri Disston & Sons, Philadelphia, Pennsylvania. This company manufactured about 20,000 items which fell into four classes:

"1. shelf or hardware goods which are sold through jobbers
   to hardware store;
2. Mill goods which go to saw mills and wood working industries;
3. Machine knife business which goes to the same market as
   the mill goods and is a direct selling proposition;
4. Milling saws, the metal cutting saws, also sold directly."

Forecasting was based on the knowledge of one's own business, its history and records of past performance, and of the knowledge of industries affecting your own. Henri Disston & Sons used maps for its forecast-

1. Committee of Industrial Planning, Boston Chamber of Commerce, "Planning
     and Production Control;" Bulletin, Vol. IX, No. 6, December 1924.
2. J. L. Stone and S. L. Kedersky, "Scientific Business Forecasting",
     Bulletin, Vol. XI, No. 2, April 1926, pp. 52-53.

ing showing the location of all kinds of timber, the location, kind and
size of saw mills, hardware stores and jobbers by state. Valuable field
work was done in cooperation with its salesmen who sent in books and
circulars on whatever location or country they might be in. The home
office furnished production, expense and sales records and charts which
were used as additional tools. [1]   The statistical department of the firm
made an intensive study of information available from the outside, such
as new building, textile mill operation, pig iron production and other
factors indicative of general business conditions. Finally, budget
control for the whole organisation was begun by the department. Fore-
casts were made fifteen months in advance, i. e., the budget for the coming year was completed in November of the current year. The present year
was projected to get the total and then an extension was made for the
next year. The estimates thus made placed emphasis, first on increasing
sales and second, on decreasing expenses. [2]

Other Advances In Management.

The principles of management have been extended beyond the field of
production.

The R. H. Macy Company in New York has a planning department organized in 1915 which occupies a purely staff position in theorganisation.
It acts in an advisory capacity to the management. The medium through
which it influences management is the Board of Operation, a body composed
of the Vice President of the Organization, the General Manager, the

1. J. L. Stone and S. L. Kedersky, "Scientific Business Forecasting"
2. Ibid., pp. 53-54. In its second part, the paper dealt with the
    technique involved in making forecasts.

Comptroller, the managers of the larger non-selling departments, and the Director of Planning. A close association exists between the Planning Department and this board so that any problems needing investigation and study can be referred to it. The Planning Department then makes recommendations resulting from such investigation directly to the board. [1] The department was, for instance, assigned the task of finding a form or method of compensation for non-selling employees in addition to their salaries which would be comparable to the commissions paid to selling employees. First it was thought best to base such a bonus on attendance, punctuality, personal rating and so forth, all of which are factors not related to production. As finally accepted, the bonus payments were limited to a payment on production measured against standards of work set for each job. Other problems on which the Planning Department made investigations and studies were those of traffic, location of selling department, design of fixtures and layout of non-selling departments in connection with the erection of a new building.

Within the past few years great advancements have been made also in time and motion study. With the use of Motion Time Analysis, improved motions have now been developed in many factories. Motion Time Analysis is a system by which the elements of a job are analyzed into fundamental body motions. It is further based on the fact that, within practical limits, the time in which a fundamental motion is performed by an expert, is a constant. Under this system, shop and factory operations can be analyzed and detailed into fundamental motions taking not more than .0007 to .005 minutes. After a job has been analyzed and classified into functional

---

1. B. Eugenia Lies, "Improving Department Store Technique"; Bulletin, Vol. X, No. 4, August 1925, p. 187.

motion groups, a series of tests are made to the classified time and motion data through which opportunities for improvements in the job are discovered. Through a further audit, the probable reduction in time on the job through the use of the necessary mechanism is found. The result is that we actually have a new job in place of the old. With the record there is a detailed description of all the motions which are "performed in balance and harmony by each member of the body." [1] The total of the time allowed for each fundamental motion will give the full time allowed for the job if performed with the specified motions. On an analysis sheet the specified motions and their proper sequence are indicated. An operation having a cycle of 1/10 minute may sometimes have several instruction sheets and the learner finds that it is difficult to picture the motion as a whole. For this reason, and in order to help him further, a motion chart is drawn on coordinate paper showing the distance to be travelled by each member of the body (usually only the hands) from the center, which is the working position, and is drawn on the abscissa, against time on the ordinate. The chart shows motions which must be performed simultaneously. The learner must be tested on his physical ability and nervous structure enabling him to perform the motions required. The analysis sheet further shows which motions are predominant, and which are mental. Some simple tests as to the fitness of the operator are made in the employment department. The learner is then instructed in the motions step by step, first by explanation, then by demonstrating in detail and letting him do the motions in accordance with the chart. The first result is usually that he works at reduced speed as he inserts unauthorized physical or mental motions. The instructor's

---

1. E. E. Brinkman, "Training for Improved Motions", American Management Association, Production Executive Series No. 70 (1928) pp. 3-8.

second task is to get the learner to eliminate all unauthorized motions.

The foreman has been defined as "the minor executive who is next in line to the working force." [1] Pains were taken to make teachers of them in sympathy with the management's point of view. Another new factor was that management realized that foremen should go through an apprenticeship.

In 1926, Cyrus McCormick, Jr. gave a definition of objectives before the United States Chamber of Commerce which are now gradually coming to be accepted. He said in part as follows:

> "Experience in industry records that the progressive, alert, keen, ambitious worker of today is the foreman of tomorrow and the executive of the future. It is obvious that management should make easy the progressive road for ambitious employees to reach the goal of real executive leadership. Foreman training involves not merely reinforcing the ability of a department head but also instructing the future executives... Correct application of company policies by men who do not make these policies is then the prime object of foremanship training... We believe in the soundness of the principle of filling all vacancies from within our organization whenever possible. We preach that whenever this proves to be impossible we ourselves have failed in a particular job of training a man for a given position." [2]

Supervisors at the Armour Company are graded on: (1) Personal qualities, (2) Intelligence, (3) Physical quality, (4) Leadership, and (5) Trade knowledge. The degree is then indicated by placing a check mark in any one of five squares showing whether he is exceptional, above average, average, below average, or poor. The rater then averages

---

1. Robert H. Spahr, "Foremanship"; Published by the United States Chamber of Commerce (1924-1925).
2. J. A. Randall and C. C. Thomason, "Foreman Training Methods", American Management Association, Production Executive Series, No. 68 (1926), p. 6.

these factors after he has rated them and weighs them mentally before determining the total of the characteristics. Consideration is also given to the employee's performance and he is again rated as either unsatisfactory, satisfactory, average, or exceptional. If he is unsatisfactory we try to find out whether he would do well in some other work. These ratings indicate the army of stand-bys in the organization who, for some reason or another, are not capable to assume greater responsibility, and yet without whom our organization could not function. [1]

The Eastman Kodak Company trains the foremen on the job on the basis of a definite plan. Department heads make it their duty to be on the look-out for exceptionally capable men who are already employed. The kinds of talent sought are then listed under such headings as Executive, Mechanical, Selling, Advertising, Administrative and others. It is also assumed by those in charge that talent may often be found engaged in the wrong kind of work. The company itself gives courses and encourages men to take courses given by outside agencies. In addition, the company has a definite plan for training men right on the job. Junior employees may temporarily be assigned to several departments and in each one they can study the department manuals and can do the regular departmental work. The head of any given department will also shift them from job to job so that the men learn the working of the department and its inter-relation with the whole organization. This program is in line with the "tendency toward a recorded system of training for each individual foreman or prospective foreman appropriate to his particular needs and accepted as such by the foreman and his responsible supervisor. The Executive trainer

---

1. Harvey G. Ellerd, "Rating Supervisors"; American Management Association, Production Executive's Series, No. 42, 1926, pp. 5-6.

takes this man, appraises his needs, and opens to him opportunities to get the training that meets his needs. The one thing that is essential to this program is the administrative technique." [1]

The North East Electric Company of Rochester has for this purpose developed a special technique, by giving students pre-foremanship courses in cooperation with other companies and the Mechanics Institute Cooperative. At the end of each month the student is required to report on the work done and the nature of instruction received, the machines operated and tools used. He is further required to give certain descriptive details and to write about the interest he has in his work. He also indicates the responsibilities assumed and he may give constructive suggestions under detailed headings. [2]

On the functions of the Board of Directors and officers of boards, it has been said that their activities were still so different, varying usually with the size of the corporation, that it is difficult to make generalizations, nor can a conclusion be drawn "because we have no definite standard to use as a method of judgment of the efficiency of the different Boards." [3]

In the machine tool industry, due to a peculiarly sensitive adjustment to the business cycle, a code of business ethics was necessary. This

1. J. A. Randall and C. C. Thomason, "Foreman Training Methods"; American Management Association, Production Executive Series, No. 68, 1928, pp. 8-9.
2. Ibid., p. 9.
3. James O. McKinsey, "Functions of Boards of Director, Board Committees and Officers", American Management Association, General Management Series No. 82, 1929.

code in part read as follows:

"1. That the 'Principles of Business Conduct' adopted by the Chamber of Commerce of the United States on May 8, 1924, be hereby adopted by the National Machine Tool Builders' Association.

"2. That this convention recommend that our members individually record their acceptance of the Principles of the Chamber of Commerce of the United States to the Association Office, on cards provided for that purpose; ....

"Code:

"1. The FOUNDATION of business is confidence; which springs from integrity, fair dealings, efficient service, and mutual benefit.— 'Goodwill' has become an indispensable asset in permanent business. Implicit confidence between producers, distributors and consumers is the bulwark of modern commerce. This requires honest effort and scrupulous accuracy in the representation of the product. The greater the business, the greater its need for confidence in order to endure.

"Annex 1. Practices Destructive of Principle 1.

1 - (A) Permitting agents, distributors or employees to conduct transactions on a lower plane of business practice than set out in this code.

1 - (B) Discrediting the equipment, product, methods or personnel of a competitor.

1 - (C) Quoting fictitiously high prices at the outset of a transaction, and lowering them without proportional changes in quantity or specifications.

1 - (D) Taking advantage of a customer's ignorance to sell him something that is not best suited to his needs.

1 - (E) Only an unethical buyer will disclose to a competitor material conditions of a competing proposal, such as price, terms, delivery, production, etc. Only an unethical competitor will procure or use such disclosures to meet competition.

"II. The REWARD of business for services rendered is a fair profit plus a safe reserve commensurate with risks involved and foresight exercised.

"Annex II. Practices destructive of Principle II....

"III. EQUITABLE CONSIDERATION is due in business alike to capital, management, employees and the public ... Annex III....

"IV. KNOWLEDGE thorough and specific—and unceasing study of the facts and forces affecting a business enterprise are essential to a lasting individual success and to efficient service to the public....

"V. PERMANENCY and continuity of service are basic aims of business, that knowledge gained may be fully utilized, confidence established and efficiency increased ....

"VII. CONTRACTS and undertakings, written or oral, are to be performed in letter and in spirit. Changed conditions do not justify their cancellation without mutual consent ....

"VIII. REPRESENTATION of goods and services should be truthfully made and scrupulously fulfilled....

"XI. UNFAIR COMPETITION embracing all acts, characterized by bad faith, deception, fraud or oppression, including commercial bribery, is wasteful, despicable and a public wrong. Business will rely for its success on the excellence of its own service." [1]

This will give a general understanding of the principles involved. The codes as adopted by many industries and trades up to this date are in all essentials the same, possible variations simply taking into account special conditions in the respective industry or trade. Generally speaking, they have been very beneficial and have greatly helped in the stabilization of certain industries.

Cooperative Approach to the Labor Problem.

The advancement made in the application of scientific management principles to factory and to business in general had its profound effect

---

1. E. F. DuBrul, "How the Machine Tool Industry's Code of Business Principles Was Developed"; American Management Association. General Management Series No. 78 (1928), pp. 8-11.

on the relationship with labor. Taylor had fought "soldiering" by
appealing to the wage motive. The period during and after the World
War taught management, however, that an appeal to the wage motive alone
was not enough to get full cooperation; more had to be done. There must
also be an appeal to the creative spirit and the service motive which
Gantt in his last years had pointed out so clearly. In its search for
new ways and means of building up a good relationship with labor, the
psychologist and economist have come to the aid of management. As a
result there has been brought about a greater cooperation between all
those affected by more efficient, or scientific management. Labor itself, at one time the most obstinate opponent of this movement, is now
realising that more efficient management is the only means by which its
own standard of living can be maintained and improved. In an address
before a joint meeting of the Taylor Society and the Management Division
of the American Society of Mechanical Engineers, William Green, President
of the American Federation of Labor, said in effect: "A full measure
of success can only be attained through the harmonious cooperation of
all productive forces in industry. To bring this about is one of the
problems of a successful manager." [1]

This short passage alone shows labor's recognition of the fundamental
necessity for cooperation and the part which management is called upon to
play. The new attitude of labor toward management is even more clearly
brought out in the following:

> "While labor is not responsible and has no voice in
> the selection or employment of management, it is vitally
> and directly interested in the quality and character of
> management.— Labor realizes that the success of manage-

---

1. William Green, "Labor's Ideals Concerning Management"; Bulletin,
   Vol. 10, No. 6, December 1925, p. 223.

ment means the success of labor.--For that reason labor
is willing to make its contribution to assist management
and to bring about the right solution of problems dealt
with by management."[1]

A few years later in 1929 the following significant statement was
made on labor's point of view at the Conference of the Labor College at
Philadelphia:

"The best regime for the development of personality
and capacity on the part of both management and employees
is one in which the psychology of conflict has been dis-
placed by common interest in working a project which is to
the mutual advantage of both parties.--The essential difference between the attitude of the worker today and the
worker even ten years ago is that the average worker now
realizes that the 'boss' is not the industry, but sees the
industry first with the boss as part of the picture.--

"Organized labor today is not merely willing to accept
a share of the responsibility for the successful conduct of
industry, but realizes that unless it does take over its
share of this burden that industry will simply not succeed
in fulfilling its primary purpose, that of providing a constantly increasing average level of different prosperity
to the great masses."[2]

Looking back on the wave of strikes during the past years we may
ask ourselves whether labor is really willing to assume its responsibility or, did the fault lie with management. There came about the
tragic realization in the autumn of 1929 and thereafter "that not enough
employers had done a good industrial relations job to safeguard us
against the philosophy of compulsion." If management would be ready to
meet labor half way, there are indications that many of the problems
could be settled and labor would actually be willing to assure its

1. William Gree, "Labor's Ideals Concerning Management"; Bulletin,
   Vol. 10, No. 6, December 1925, p. 244.
2. T. G. Spates, "Analysis of Industrial Relations Trend" (Conference
   of the Labor College at Philadelphia); American Management Association, Personnel Series, No. 25 (1929).

responsibility. A more recent utterance to this effect is that of
William Allen White, who at the recent International Management Congress (1938) drew attention to the responsibility of industry and management
in solving the problem of unemployment. At the same meeting, Robert J.
Watt, American Workers' Delegate to the International Labor Office,
told his audience consisting of about 1,000 business executives, bhat
industry would have discipline and responsibility as "soon as you stop
waging war against unions and give your workers a chance to develop
their own pattern of union discipline and responsibility.— American
labor wants to be recognized as the partner of capital in production,
as the customer of capital in distribution, as the majority voice in
a political democracy and as the substantial center of our community
life." [1]   In spite of all the unrest, the last years have brought about
positive results, especially when we consider that labor is speaking
in terms of cooperation rather than conflict. Spates, in his paper
"Analysis of Industrial Relation Trend", mentioned the following incident: Some time ago an executive of a large industry gave a talk in
New York on the development of industrial relations. When he had finished
his speech he said:

> "Gentlemen, the surprise to us has been that all of these
> things (and he named stabilization of employment, vacation,
> extra compensation, etc.) have cost us nothing. (He mentioned
> as an illustration of that point) We have had no labor dif-
> ficulties. (And after having said that, he hesitated and added)
> Just a minute. A few months ago we had a flare up in one of
> our plants. We made an investigation, found that management
> was at fault, corrected the condition, and everything since
> then has been satisfactory." [2]

1. International Management Congress. New York Times. September 21, 1938.
2. T. G. Spates, op. cit., p. 19.

To be effective, scientific management must be based on cooperation between the planner, the foreman and the worker. Labor unions are now using the stop-watch and other instruments for proper investigation of the time it takes to finish a given job, in order to be able to confront employers with FACTS.

The opposition of labor became less and less when the report of the Committee on the Elimination of Waste in Industry was published. Labor leaders hailed this report as being one of the most important documents in their favor, for it placed the greatest responsibility for the elimination of waste on the management. What is at least equally important is that the Committee had been largely composed of Taylor's men. Of course, the report mentioned labor's responsibilities along with those of the management, but it also pointed the way in which many of the labor controversies could be eliminated. Scientific management is nothing else than an attempt to place management on a factual basis, and knowing the facts is a great step towards the solution of labor problems. This has been more and more recognized during this period. On the other hand, it is quite possible that more could have been done in regard to stock ownership by employees. Stock ownership by management has proved to be of great benefit to the organization, would it not also be beneficial to have labor share in the profits of the corporation? Would it not help to create greater willingness on the part of labor to assume its own responsibilities? It would certainly help in bettering the conditions of the workingman. We should not forget what Taylor said on this score:

"	"... if the result of my work were merely to increase dividends of the manufacturing companies, I certainly should not devote my time to this object. Scientific management is

for me, then, primarily a means of bettering the conditions
of the working people." [1]

Since even labor is now looking towards a factual basis in its
relationship with management, objections against collective bargaining seem to be decreasing. In this connection we should remember Taylor's
position which was as follows:

> "... in many establishments under the ordinary system,
> collective bargaining has become and is in my judgment an
> absolute necessity." [2]

Taylor pointed out "under the ordinary system." Why should collective bargaining not also be possible under scientific management? Since
labor itself wants to know the facts, there can hardly be any objection.
Today the individual worker wants to know what constitutes a fair day's
work.

> "The workman has constantly in his mind what is a fair
> and honest day's work, and you can't set wages by time study
> or by any other scientific method that does not take into
> consideration the worker's judgment of fairness in this
> thing. You have got to measure that. This is one of the
> elements, and if you leave that out you haven't a proper wage;
> because, no matter how scientifically you measure it, he is
> going to give the day's work that he conceives fair and
> honest and he is no more dishonest than the managers are.
> He has his idea of justice and fair dealing in a day's work,
> and the managers have their ideas of justice. A really
> scientific method of fixing wages is one that will put to-
> gether the management's idea of a fair rate and the workman's
> idea of a fair rate, and I don't see any other method of
> doing that except through collective bargaining." [3]

It was not until the time of the first National Conference on Unem-

ployment in New York (February 1914), that the attitude towards the

---

1. Hearings before the Special Committee of the House of Representatives
   to Investigate the Taylor and Other Systems of Shop Management,
   pp. 1459, 1462.
2. Ibid., p. 1444.
3. Wm. R. Leiserson, "The Workers Reaction to Scientific Management,"
   Bulletin, Vol. 5, No. 4, August 1920, p. 164.

unemployment problem assumed definite form. At that time Professor
Seager, Chairman of the Conference and President of the American
Association for Labor Legislation, said on the question of what should
be done in the United States:

> "The aspect of the question most impressed upon my own
> thought was the necessity of regularizing employment. It is
> still true that nine out of ten employers employ and dis-
> charge their wage-earners with very little consideration for
> the welfare of the wage-earner."[1]

Gradually the idea of regularizing employment became an important
aspect of the problem. In 1916 the Ontario Commission on Unemployment
made the following suggestion on how this could be accomplished:

> "Employers may largely regularize their staffs of
> workers (1) by improved method of employment and training,
> which will lessen the present 'turnover' of employees; (2)
> by adding new lines of products to ensure greater continuity
> of employment; (3) by standardizing a portion of products,
> thereby making it feasible to manufacture for stock more
> largely in slack seasons; (4) by securing orders from cus-
> tomers longer in advance than is now the practice, so that
> the factory output may be made more uniform, and (5) by
> developing export trade..."[2]

During and after the War, special attention was called to the increasing turnover in labor; to the percentage of turnover as well as to
the problem of reducing it. So far as personnel departments are concerned,
many of them had been created on a welfare basis rather than on the
basis of sound business. Hence, when the 1920-1921 depression came and
management was forced to make curtailments, they reduced their personnel
departments or closed them completely. As another step towards greater
economy, wages were cut drastically. All this led business to a process
of self-analysis and to inquiries into the soundness of both philosophy

1. American Labor Legislation, Rev., p. 311, May 1914.
2. Report, Ontario Commission on Unemployment, p. 12; quoted also in
   E. E. Hunt, Scientific Management Since Taylor, p. 174.

and technique of personnel relation and to extensive revaluation of personnel policies and practice. [1]   These research activities resulted in the establishment by organised labor of the Labor Bureau, Inc., the Workers Education Bureau of America, the Personnel Research Federation and the Industrial Relations Section of Princeton University. Similar sections were later established at the University of Michigan and at Stanford University in California [2] and since that time at many other universities.

In the Spring of 1927, the Central Labor Union and Labor College of Philadelphia held a two-day conference which had as its purpose the bringing about of better cooperation between management and labor, especially with a view to developing better methods of production. Scientific management engineers and executives participated actively at this conference, with the result that similar meetings were held at Cleveland and other places. In 1928 at Cleveland, the ladies garment workers and their employers agreed upon measured standards of output, based on time and motion studies. In some of the railroads, the Baltimore and Ohio and the Canadian National, cooperation between management and workers for the introduction of better methods has been organized and the workers themselves have on their payroll an engineer who makes studies on improved methods. [3]

Industrial Relations.

During the War, L. F. Loree of the Delaware and Hudson Railroad, directed that a man be selected whose sole duty would be to study

1. T. G. Spates, "Analysis of Industrial Relations Trend" (Conference of the Labor College at Philadelphia); American Management Association, Personnel Series No. 25 (1929), pp. 7-8
2. Ibid., p. 8.
3. The Taylor Society (H. S. Person, Editor) , "Scientific Management in American Industry"; New York, 1929, p. 21.

employment relations. From this evolved gradually a Personnel Department with a force of about thirty people. This department is now correlated to all other departments of the road. In 1920 a new body was created to be known as the Board of Disciplining Officers of the Delaware & Hudson Company. This board was to consider such matters as discipline, wages, interpretation of agreements and other matters relating to labor. The seven members on this board represent the major departments of the road and are of the grade of superintendents. The board has a non-voting chairman and secretary. Through this board, prompt adjustments of minor grievances has been brought about. It has also helped in avoiding dissatisfaction and has tended to create a good feeling among employees. It means an "open door" to employees through which they can call attention to all possible irregularities. So far as the clerical force is concerned the road has also introduced a more intimate study of man and job analysis. [1]

The Standard Oil Company of California was one of the first industrial companies in the United States to make a statement on employer-employee relations policies (May 1923). This statement was printed in book form with the subtitle: "Discussion of the Relationship Between Personnel and Management of the Standard Oil Company of California." A similar statement was issued by the Western Electric Company on Relations with Employees (1924). It states the relationship under headings as:

"To pay all employees adequately for services rendered.

"To maintain reasonable hours of work and safe working conditions...."

---

1. W. W. Bates, "Personnel Activities of the Delaware and Hudson Railroad" Bulletin, Vol. XI, No. 2, April 1926.

In 1925 there appeared a statement by the Bell Telephone System outlining their personnel policy and giving "three fundamental lines of action", the first of which reads:

> "1. Remove from every company, department and office practice, policy, custom, routine, phrase and tradition which is inconsistent with each individual's feeling that he is a part of the enterprise or which barks back to the old master and servant conception that a contract is the only tie between the individual employee and the company." [1]

One of the latest statements on personnel policy issued in 1935 is on the "Employee Relationship Policy of the Tennessee Valley Authority." The most interesting provision is probably contained in the following statement:

> "Employment in a position is not a vested right to be retained primarily because of possession, but only if quality of service justifies continuance of employment." [2]

Recent tendencies in all fields of employment have been towards a further reduction of working hours. Some years ago, a Western railroad made experiments along these lines by having billers work for six hours without intermission. It was found that they produced as much work as those working eight hours with the usual one hour lunch period. Short shifts will bring about a greater utilisation of office building and the whole equipment for a longer time during the day. As far as employees are concerned, it will no doubt help to put greater emphasis on piece-work and bonus plans as a method of clerical compensation.

---

1. T. G. Spate. "Analysis of Industrial Relations Trend": American Management Association. Personnel Series, No. 25, pp. 16-17.
2. Ibid., pp. 17-18.

The minimum requirements of the functions which an office has to perform has been called the "number of clerical man hours."[1]   If the staff is reduced beyond a given point, it will mean the elimination of some activities. While management has the prerogative in demanding a reduction in the office force, it must by the same token also accept the consequences. Today an office manager must be able to express the minimum requirements of office activities in terms of clerical man hours, or else he may find himself in an embarrassing position.

Long before the National Security Act was passed, the Eastman Kodak Company had a program of unemployment insurance known as the "Rochester Unemployment Benefit Plan." The plan provided for the building up of a reserve beginning with 1931, and the payment of benefits after January 1, 1933. The Eastman Kodak Company has for this purpose set aside a reserve fund to which it made yearly contributions of $100,000. Payments were made in accordance with the provisions of the plan, beginning January 1, 1933. Eligible for benefit payments were those working less than half time and those who were laid off. The maximum payment per week was $18, payable for a period of 13 weeks during any one year.[2]

The period of compulsory legislation was ushered in with the passage, by the State of Wisconsin, of their unemployment insurance law in 1932. It marked a fundamental and radical change in the national trend of industrial relations. It should be remembered that even organized labor was against the use of the legislative machinery in attaining its goals. It was not until the fall of 1932, at the Convention of the American Federation of Labor, that a position in favor of legislative action was taken by organized labor.[3]

1. F. T. Roland, "Present Status and Probable Future Trend in Office Management"; American Management Association. Office Management Series, No. 61 (1933), p. 9.
2. John B. Black, M. B. Folsom and others, "Practical Aspects of Unemployment Insurance and Old Age Security", Personnel Series No. 23 (1936).
3. T. G. Spates, op. cit., p. 14

During the War, the unions had a peak membership of about 5,000,000 members. In 1929 they had not more than 3,400,000. Through Section 7A and other encouragement given to organized labor by the Federal Government, union membership was about 4,000,000 by the end of 1936. In drawing his conclusions, Spates stated:

> "... after twenty five years of reasonably intelligent and active effort on the part of organized labor leaders they have been able to persuade not more than eleven out of 100 of America's wofkmen to join and pay dues to trade unions.— If, after twenty-five and even more years, trade union leaders have been able to persuade only eleven out of a hundred American workmen to join, then I think it is reasonable to conclude that the normal thing for the American workman is not to join a trade union. If the normal thing for him to do is not to join, then when he takes the abnormal action, namely, signs up with a union, I think the least that can be done is to try to find out the reason why, and place the responsibility where it really belongs."[1]

The scientific management movement started with emphasis on piece-rates which later gave way to the different methods of bonus payments or hourly wages with premiums. In 1926 the Manufacturers' Research Association of Massachusetts made an unprejudiced study of the wage problem, advocating the following principles:

"1. Piece Work:

"A. The M.R.A. (stands for the Manufacturers' Research Association) Wage Payment Plan would insist on standardised shop methods prior to time-study.

"B. The M. R. A. Wage Payment Plan would insist that production rates be set only on the basis of accurate time-study.

"C. In order to make it possible to measure and compare the efficiency of operators and departments, the establishment of a definite task becomes at once desirable. For a good average worker the attainment of this task would represent 100 per cent efficiency.

---

1. T. G. Spates, op. cit., p. 18.

"D. The M.R.A. Wage Payment Plan would guarantee a daywork
rate for operators in all cases where the worker is
unable to perform this task on account of conditions
beyond his control. It would charge these excess
costs to the proper expense account and distribute
them together with other overhead charges.

"E. The M.R.A. Wage Payment Plan would establish definite
breaking-in periods for new operators.

"F. The M.R.A. Wage Payment Plan would provide instruction
cards prescribing the exact condition under which all
operators should work; i.e., feeds, speeds, number of
pieces per hour, set-up time, etc. In addition to these
cards there would also be rate cards showing the base
rate and the amount of production an operator must turn
out in order to obtain these rates.

"G. The M.R.A. Wage Payment Plan would advocate paying a
flat reward to any operator who presented an improved
method for performing a task, after which it would
recommend that a new rate be established for performing
the task in accordance with the new method.

"H. The M.R.A. Wage Payment Plan would provide and maintain
accurate records of production and scrap. Whenever it is
possible to do so, it would pay a bonus for minimum scrap.

"I. The M.R./. Wage Payment Plan would provide that a weekly
ANALYSIS SHEET be made up from the reports turned in.
This would permit executives to obtain direct control of
labor costs.

"J. Under this plan of wage payment the task of all indirect
workers are studied and the proper ratio of direct to
indirect labor established for each department.

"K. If it is so desired, a bonus may be paid to indirect
workers, based on the ratio of direct to indirect labor
hours in any given department, established in the manner
described in the preceding paragraph. The exact method
of computing this bonus, and the time interval between
any two payments thereof should be determined by the
management of any company in such a way as to satisfy
the needs and requirements of the particular business." [1]

---

1. A. B. Rich, "Principles of Wage Payment"; Bulletin, Vol. XI, No. 4,
October 1926, pp. 214-218.

The National Cash Register Company had for many years to a limited extent used "gang piece-work." In the automobile industry, the company also used the decimal hour in expressing basic standards. Now the standards are expressed in money. The objectives of the group payment plan were as follows:

1. To reduce labor cost,
2. Increase earnings of workers,
3. Maintain quality,
4. Simplify the clerical system,
5. Reduce stock in process,
6. Create cooperative leaders,
7. Maintain individual incentives,
8. Help new employees,
9. Develop leaders, and
10. Reduce overhead cost. [1]

In its first trial, the company used the Packard Plan. For the handling of stock it was soon found that under the incentive of group payment the work, formerly done by seven men, could be handled by four who received wages of about five men. The Automatic Screw Machine Department where formerly day-work had been the basis of wage payments was next in line for a change to group payment. In this case, the group, consisting of 100 men, proved to be too large to develop a common interest and they did not earn a bonus for several months. Through further experiments with several small groups, the company was able to see advantages and disadvantages of the group payment method. Out of this experience the company developed what was called the "Time Basis Plan." The principles of this plan are as follows:

1. Standards expressed in decimal hours per 100 units and based upon Time Study.

2. The performance of an average experienced worker, having knowledge of the job and working at normal effort under good conditions we considered was 75 per cent efficient.

---

1. R. F. Whisler and others, "Group Versus Individual Incentive"; American Management Association; Production Executive Series No. 73 (1928).

3. Bonus started after attaining 75 per cent efficiency, 1 per cent bonus was paid for each 1 per cent in excess of 75 per cent efficiency.

4. This is a gain sharing plan, the company receiving one-fourth, of the actual increase above 75 per cent. For example, to raise the efficiency from 75 per cent to 100 per cent requires 33 1/3 per cent increase in output but will pay 25 per cent bonus.

5. Efficiency is the ratio of the group output to the group in--put, in hours.

6. Members of the group are given guaranteed rates, graduated according to their individual skill, speed, responsibilities and relative value to the other group members. Individual rates are adjusted at intervals as needed ....

7. . . . . .

8. Where more than one operation is done on a part or assembly by a group, one standard covers all work.

9. Groups are credited with accepted work; reoperation is on their own time.

10. Group bonus on inspection work contains a quality allowance. If this is exceeded, the group suffers a penalty and if rejections are below standard allowance, a bonus is earned in addition to that for quantity of output.[1]

In using this plan the company met with difficulties in figuring employees. With the cost system, the costs were subject to changes in individual rates and fluctuated with group efficiency. Hence, the plan had to be modified and this new plan was called the "Money Basis Plan." The two important changes were:

1. Changed basis of bonus from 75 per cent to 100 per cent-- eliminating the gain sharing features.

2. Replaced time standards with equivalent value expressed in money--corrected to 100 per cent basis for earning bonus.

This plan seems to have worked better. Further experience showed that the plan was beneficial where group efforts were necessary, as in

1. R. F. Whisler and others, "Group Versus Individual Incentive," pp. 9-10.
2. Ibid, p. 11.

the handling of material, progressive assembling and similar work.
Workers who do the same operation have been successfully placed on
group work. One of the most essential requirements is the development
of a common interest. Another factor for success was the establishment of a proper rate base. Some firms use one rate for new workers,
and once they have learned the job they are placed on the advanced
rate which the other workers of the group receive. As in the case of
individual bonus payments, the standards are all based on time and
motion study, and in establishing these standards, an average worker
using normal skill and effort is used. From the standards obtained
through time and motion studies, the National Cash Register Company
derives either bonus standard times in hours or money standard in
prices per 100 parts. The task is then set at 80 per cent of standard
and the man is guaranteed his base rate or wages regardless of whether
he reaches the standard. The bonus is "one per cent over his base rate
for each per cent increase in his production over the task rate."

Another form of bonus payment is predetermined profit sharing for
managers and executives. There exists some difference of opinion as to
whether such bonus should be paid in cash or in stock. In the 1928-1929
era in over 70 per cent of the cases the bonus was fully paid in cash.
In 77 per cent of the plans the bonus payment was made annually, while
in 11 per cent of the cases payment was deferred and then mostly paid
in stock. The companies doing this hoped by this means to keep the turnover of their managerial group down. The E. I. du Pont de Nemours & Co.
and the General Motors Corporation are using the latter method.

One method takes into consideration that the common stockholders
have a right in the earning power of the company in addition to the assets

and, therefore, after interest on bonds and dividends for preferred
stock are deducted, a certain percentage of the present value of the
common stock is set aside. This method was used by the Leeds and
Northrup Company. Some base the deduction simply on the par value of
the common stock, but if the market value appreciates considerably the
method tends to become somewhat unfair to the stockholders.[1]

At first one might think that every one of the managerial staff
should be included in the distribution of the fund. In practice this
does not hold. Since the percentage of profit going to the fund is
fixed, those who share in its distribution must feel confident that
every newcomer will pay his own way through added initiative on his
part. For a similar reason, the higher executives are usually given
a larger part of the fund because the contribution they make to managerial ability is proportionately larger.[2] Bonus payments in the form
of profit sharing are usually most effective when applied to a small
group within a large organisation such as the managerial staff. For
the rank and file it is only effective in comparatively small industrial
companies.

The Diebold Safe and Lock Company deducts each month from net
earnings a certain amount for dividends on the common, after which a
percentage of the remainder is set aside for the executives and key
men in the organization. The division is made by an executive committee
elected by the Board of Directors. The heads of the Finance, Sales and
Production units together with the President of the company determine
the key men in each division. From the report it seems that even some

1. C. O. Balderstone, "A Cross Section of Current Practice with Profit
Sharing" (The Technique of Basing Extra Compensation of Managers
and Executives on Profits), American Management Association,
General Management Series, No. 84 (1929), p. 11.
2. Ibid. p. 13.

industrial workers in key positions were included in the plan. Once
a man is placed on the list of those who share in the profit, he is
immediately informed of it and thereafter no change is made without
first consulting him. Each month the men on the list get a letter
informing them of the results of the past month and telling them what
the management hopes to accomplish in the future. Of an organization
having about 450 men, 20 foremen, and from 10 to 15 others (department
heads) participated. Some of the results were: Costs were reduced,
there was greater cooperation between the different units and divisions,
a greater interest manifested itself as to the condition of the company.
Since the adoption of the plan, the company moved from fourth to second
place in the industry.[1]

Out of 65 cases investigated, only four plans were dropped because
of dissatisfaction. Most of the plans were more than five years old.
These plans were usually definite as to deductions from earnings and
percentage of profits to be placed in the fund.

In 1920 there were from 15,000 to 20,000 employees in the clothing
industry in Rochester. From the technical point of view the industry
was still highly disorganized. On the other hand, labor as well as the
employers were organized in their opposition to each other. Then an
agreement was entered into between employers and employees which recognizes the right of the management to introduce changes in the technique
of manufacture so long as the welfare of the workers is not endangered.

---

1. Weible, H. C., "Managerial Profit Sharing in the Diebold Safe and Lock
   Company" (The Technique...op. cit.), American Management Association,
   General Management Series, No. 84 (1929), pp. 23-25.

It further recognizes the right of continuous production. The strike was outlawed and management in turn gave up the use of the lockout as a weapon in industrial warfare. Back of the whole undertaking was the idea of labor management. The labor managers were given the task of shaping labor policies in the market and administering them in the different factories.[1]

The agreement represents, so to speak, the Constitution for the clothing industry in Rochester. The interpretation of this Constitution is left to a Labor Adjustment Board made up of union officials and labor managers. This Board meets once each week and is presided over by an Impartial Chairman who acts as an umpire or industrial judge and is paid by both sides. Questions which came before this Board were on what constitutes a proper piece rate for a given operation, on what constitutes a fair production standard for a weekly wage and similar problems.[2] Probably the greatest advantage of the functioning of this machinery is that those who operate it are in close touch with both sides of the rank and file of the industry.

There are employees representation plans of various types usually made to fit local conditions. Of these, the "advisory" plan is probably the most common. One of the plans indicative of the good intention of management states:

> "The employees and the management of the company undertake by adoption of this plan of an industrial council to establish their relations upon a definite and durable basis of mutual understanding and confidence. To this end the employees and management shall have equal representation in the consideration of all questions of policy/relation to

---

1. Meyer Jacobstein, "Can Industrial Democracy be Efficient?" Bulletin, Vol. V, No. 4, August 1920, pp. 153-155 (reprinted in Hunt, pp. 212-221.)
2. Ibid, p. 155.

working conditions, health, safety, hours of labor, wages, recreation, education, and other similar matters of interest.

"As the principal means of carrying this plan into effect, there shall be organized an industrial council composed of representatives of employees and representatives of the management... both of whom shall have at all times equal voice and voting power in considering matters coming before the council. Through this council any employee or group of employees, or the management, may at any time present suggestions, requests, or matter requiring adjustment with a certainty of full and fair hearing."[1]

Under this plan, if the vote in the council should remain a tie, the matter shall be referred to the president of the company who shall then either propose a settlement, or take further steps to bring about an adjustment.

In addition to the advisory type of employees' representation plans, we find the "government" type of plan. Under this plan there is a House of Representatives composed of elected representatives of employees, and a Senate composed of supervisors and minor executives. The cabinet is made up of the president and other higher officials of the company. Sometimes the House of Representatives and the Senate are combined. Under the "Joint Committee" type there are many variations. Committees are formed, usually along departmental lines, consisting of management and employees representatives. A joint committee deals with matters which are beyond the jurisdiction of any given department.[2]

The plans of some companies include other activities as, for instance, mutual benefit associations, a savings fund, a safety committee, a social and educational club and the like. Sometimes cooperative associations began without any thought on employee representation, but the

1. Chicago Conference: "Employee Representation Technique," American Management Association, Production Exec. Series No. 49 (1926), p. 4.
2. Ibid, p. 5.

latter feature was later included and the machinery for representation
was set up by simply expanding the existing organization. One association
has a plan of lmited employees' representation; the extent of its powers
may be seen from the following provision:

> "The purpose of the association is to prevent the enforce-
> ment by the management of unjust rules affecting the discipline
> and working conditions of employees, to prevent unjust discharges
> or removals of employees, to inaugurate, when needed, new rules
> affecting the discipline, work or conditions of work of employees,
> to conduct the social and so-called welfare activities of the
> company without dictation, but with the cooperation of the manage-
> ment."[1]

In the preparation of an employee representation plan some guiding
principles should be observed such as:

> "1. The object of the plan should be clearly defined so that
> there is no doubt as to its intent and purposes.
>
> 2. The organization of agencies for carrying out the prin-
> ciples set forth should be stated in no uncertain terms;
> language should be used that is easily understood by the
> least educated employee.
>
> 3. The duties and powers of these agencies for representa-
> tion should be consistent with the purpose of the plan.
>
> 4. The method of procedure agreed upon should be such as
> to provide the most effective contact between manage-
> ment and employees.
>
> 5. The provisions for amendment should be ample and permit
> such changes as were proved necessary by experience."[2]

In all such plans, provisions for proper representation for supervisors should not be left out. A manager of industrial relations is
usually charged with the duty of administering the plan, in some companies
an assistant to the president, or a special assistant is given this responsibility. Special consideration must be given to branch plants; in the

---

1. Chicago Conference: "Employee Representation Technique," American
   Management Association, Production Exec. Series No. 49 (1926), p. 6.
2. Ibid, p. 7.

case of large branches, departmental councils and a general joint council has been found necessary in order to deal with all the problems which might arise. Where there are small groups of employees in many locations the "joint committee" type of plan seems to have worked best.[1]

The American Multigraph Company has an employee representation plan which may be considered as falling under the "advisory" type. The president of the company, however, has no authority to dispose or adjust (for) any matter calling for arbitration. The rules and regulations of the plan have the following provisions:

> "In event cabinet and congress are unable to reach an agreement on any change in policy affecting wages, working hours and conditions, the president shall appoint a committee from the cabinet to act with a like number of congressmen appointed by the chairman of congress; this committee to constitute an arbitration board. The president, or in his absence, a vice-president, shall preside over this board without vote. A majority vote of this board shall find both the employees and the company in matters coming within their jurisdiction. In case this board cannot reach an agreement the matter in question shall be referred to the board of directors for decision."[2]

The Standard Oil Company of New Jersey has an employee representation plan in operation since 1918, embracing seven refineries, the marketing territory of the parent company and the producing fields of its subsidiaries. The plan is of the "joint committee" type. The Joint Agreement of the company reads:

Purposes and Scope.

> This agreement makes provision whereby elected representatives of the employees shall meet in joint conference with representatives of the management to discuss and to settle, subject to final review by the Board of Directors, all matters of joint interest, such as hours, wages, working conditions and the adjustment of grievances."[3]

---

1. Chicago Conference: "Employee Representation Technique," pp. 8-10.
2. Ibid, pp. 11-12.
3. Ibid, pp. 16-17.

This shows the wide scope of the agreement. The basis of representation varies between the different plants depending on local conditions in the marketing and producing fields. In the larger refineries there may be one representative for each 150 men, while in smaller places there may be one representative for each 25 men. The plan was placed in operation at a time of industrial peace and without demand on the part of the employees. The scope of the whole agreement may further be seen from the headings of the other parts. These are: (2) Annual Elections; (3) Joint Conference; (4) Wage Adjustments; (5) Right of Appeal; and (6) Non-Discrimination.

These meetings have been of great benefit since they provided free and frank discussions by the employee representatives, and questions on company policies could be answered in terms of their own language.

On the question of "What Managerial Problems Should Be Discussed in Joint Representation Meetings," H. L. Badger, general manager of the Bell Telephone Company, Pennsylvania, gave the following as some typical classes of problems discussed in committees:

Wage problems are approached along these lines:

> "a. Is the wage fundamentally correct?
> b. Is the employee's share in the revenue of the company correct?
> c/ Is the basis of distribution of the wage as scientific as it
>   can be with the facts that are known?"[1]

By approaching the wage problem in such a way, it will necessitate the discussion of a wide range of company affairs in order to be convincing. Other problems coming for discussion may be on working practices and conditions; questions on a thrift plan, if the company has one; in

---

1. Chicago Conference: "Employee Representation Technique," p. 44
   (From the discussion on "What Managerial Problems Should Be
   Discussed in Joint Representation Meetings.")

the case of utility companies it is also necessary to keep the personnel advised of certain company policies and objectives.

Management and Education.

Henry P. Kendall of the Plimpton Press, Norwood, Massachusetts, first classified the types of management. To Kendall, the simplest types of management fall under three heads:

    I. Unsystematized Management.
    II. Systematized Management.
    III. Scientific Management.

The functions of all three types of management as given above are:

    A. Accounting.
    B. Purchasing.
    C. Storage of Materials.
    D. Execution of Work.
    E. Efficiency of Workers.[1]

It is along these lines that education in management has been developed, although the names of the functions may have been changed and many new functions added. In 1926 the Bulletin of the Taylor Society listed a "Nucleus of a Management Library with Emphasis on Scientific Management," which the Society recommends to its members.[2] Not only is the number of books (about 120) surprisingly large, but from the educational point of view the arrangement is of special interest since it shows how broad the subject has become and how far specialization has gone in education. The list of books is subdivided into the following sections:

    1. Background.
    2. Taylor Classics.
    3. Elementary Discussion of Management.

---

1. The Amos Tuck School: Addresses and Discussions At the Conference on Scientific Management, held October 12, 13, 14, 1911; Dartmouth College, Hanover, N. H., 1912, p. 113.
2. Bulletin, Vol. XI, No. 4, October 1926, pp. 224 ff.

4. Scientific Management General Treatment.
5. Application of Scientific to Special Industries.
6. Scientific Management; Special Phases.
7. Office Management.
8. Purchasing.
9. Business Policy.
10. Budget Control, Forecasting and Regularization.
11. Managerial Accounting.
12. Financial Management.
13. Statistical and Graphical Methods.
14. Sales Management.
15. Retail Store Management.
16. Personnel Administration and Labor Policy.
17. Psychologic Background of Management.
18. Economic Background of Management.

The need for special courses in general management and particularly in scientific management became apparent after the rate-advance
hearings in 1910. The following year the Conference on Scientific
Management at the Amos Tuck School of Administration and Finance at
Dartmouth College took place. It showed that the universities began
to recognize the role they would have to play in the management movement which was well under way by this time. Teaching and practice from
then on went hand in hand and colleges and universities willingly assumed their part in leadership. In this development Taylor had assigned
them a definite task. "What we are looking for," he said, "is the
ready-made, competent man whom someone else had trained." Management
has an extremely wide diversity of methods. It is here that all those
practicing management should contribute to the store of knowledge, while
the colleges and universities in turn are the proper places where such
knowledge can be disseminated. This in turn will help to bring about a
common practice and a general acceptance of known scientific management
principles. Business has not only grown in size, but also in complexity.
Under such conditions it is of importance that the man in a responsible

position should have full knowledge of both principles and practice, and should use only what has proved to be scientifically the best in management. Part of the complexity of modern business has been brought about through the rapid advances in technique; these advances have in fact been more rapid during the last decades than at any other period. These technical advances in turn force management to depend more than ever on faculties which have to be developed through some sort of academic training. Management needs men who have a store of knowledge acquired by study and are, therefore, able to apply this knowledge with that natural ability which such training has given them. This means professional, scientific training. It puts the manager on the same footing with the professional man; as a matter of fact, it makes him a professional man. Thus the manager will have scientific training because management is a science. However, since management is not only a science but also an art, he will need experience and will have to depend on it the same way as a medical man does. Experience will be the training in the art. Like any other professional man, the manager of today needs both, one supplementing the other.

Functional management makes this training even more imperative. Taylor has drawn attention to this fact, and even has gone as far as to help young men to get that training. The manager around whom all these functional activities turn must at least know what his subordinates are trying to accomplish. Nor is a factory a self-contained unit as it has been at an earlier period. Management of today is in constant relations with unions, trade organizations and boards, labor relations boards, industrial research institutes, employers' associations, the state boards, state and federal agencies and the like. Under the circumstances it is only natural that education should have made advancements in keeping with the demands made from the men who have gone through training courses in management.

Many of the things that have been accomplished in education have been mentioned before. During the World War, Mr. Cooke as Chairman of the War Industries Board, guided the development of courses in the handling of stores at ten American colleges.[1] College and university courses in management have increased tremendously. Both the number of institutions giving courses and the number of courses actually offered have increased. The following institutions had, in 1912, but one course in management of an engineering grade, but ten years later each had eight:[2]

Columbia University.
Massachusetts Institute of Technology.
New York University.
Pennsylvania State College.
Purdue University.
University of Kansas.
University of Pittsburgh.
Yale University —Sheffield Scientific School.

The Harvard School of Business Practice, along with other colleges and universities, is collecting data upon which a concrete science of management is being built.

Professional Organizations.

In addition to the many colleges and universities which are collecting data and sharing the knowledge thus acquired, there are many societies and professional groups which do essentially the same thing. Of these there are so many that we can only mention the most important organizations.

---

1. H. B. Drury, Scientific Management, Rev. and Enl. Edition, New York, 1922, p. 188.
2. L. P. Alford, Ten Year's Progress in Management. A paper presented during the management week, October 16-21, 1922, A. S. M. E. Transactions, (pp. 1243-1296), p. 1256.

The oldest organization is the American Society of Mechanical Engineers to which Taylor had presented all his papers. But once the scientific management movement was well under way, the Taylor Society, first organized as the Society to Promote the Science of Management (formally organized on December 4, 1911), became the leading exponent of the scientific management and efficiency movement.

After Taylor's death on December 11, 1915, its name was changed to the Taylor Society. The Society held meetings three or four times a year, which were attended by many non-members. The Bulletin of the Society soon became the leading source of material covering the movement. During 1918 the Bulletin was suspended and there was little activity at the Society. In December 1918, however, a group of members gathered at Washington to discuss its future. During the same month a meeting of the Governing Board was held and it decided that:

1. The activities of the Society be extended and intensified;
2. The membership be increased to represent all that is best in management engineering;
3. The affairs of the Society be placed in charge of a Managing Director;
4. The Society establish permanent headquarters in New York;
5. The Constitution of the Society be revised.[1]

The Society also maintains a management library for its members. It has published from time to time lists of books on scientific management. Under the leadership of Harlow S. Person, the Society published "Scientific Management in American Industry"[2] in 1929, which constitutes the best work extant on scientific management and is "a summary of a decade's study, analysis and exposition of the philosophy, principles

---

1. Bulletin of the Taylor Society, Vol. IV, No. 2, April 1919.
2. Harper and Brothers, New York and London, 1929.

and procedures of scientific management; and a picture of it s status and influence today."[1]

On May 26, 1917, the Society of Industrial Engineers with headquarters in Chicago was formed. This society had as its object the bringing together in one body the Taylor followers as well as the rival parties and groups which had arisen at that time. Its purpose was to coordinate the efficiency movement and during the World War its special purpose was that of aiding the Government. Until 1936 the Taylor Society and the Society of Industrial Engineers existed side by side. In 1936 the two societies merged to form the Society for the Advancement of Management, Inc., and the "Journal" superseded the Bulletin of the Taylor Society.

Although at present inactive, mention should be made of the Frederick W. Taylor Cooperators, an institute which was formed after Taylor's death. Its purpose was to continue to extend the Taylor system; to gather material for a biography, which had been accomplished in 1923, with the publication of Copley's "Frederick W. Taylor, Father of Scientific Management;" to provide a clearing house for information touching on scientific management; and to collect books, data, and memorabilia. The cooperators were Carl G. Barth, Morris L. Cooke, H. K. Hathaway and James M. Dodge. The latter died, however, during the year of the formation of this institution. Its advisory board included all those who had been the more immediate followers of Taylor in the United States and abroad.

The management movement has not remained within these organizations mentioned. More general institutions of American thought and action are now championing and developing Taylor's work, such as the Federated American Engineering Societies and other engineering groups, the Chamber

---

1. Harper and Brothers, New York and London, 1929, p. xv. (Foreword by Henry P. Kendall.)

of Commerce of the United States, and many leading technical and engineering journals. It is also helped by the Department of Commerce and other Government bodies.

Of more recent date is the American Management Association with its manifold activities. After the depression of 1921 and the organization of the different bureaus on Industrial Relations, such as the Princeton Industrial Relations Section, the Labor Bureau, etc., management had a different concept which is best expressed in the following words:

> "... if money, material and equipment are available to all my competitors on equal terms, then the most potential source of advantage that I have is a more effective utilization of human resources through the technique of personnel administration."[1]

This meant the beginning of a new philosophy of industrial relations which had been gradually developed through trial and error from the period of the World War. This development brought about the formation of the American Management Association. The origin of this organization springs from two fields of organized industrial work, the "Corporation Schools" and the "National Association of Employment Managers." Those engaged in the field of "Corporation Schools" had organized their activities on a national basis in 1913, through the formation of the National Association of Corporation Schools. In 1920 they incorporated as the National Association of Corporation Training. Local employment management groups had been started as early as 1913, but it was not until 1918 that the National Association of Employment Managers was founded. In 1920, the Association was incorporated under the name of Industrial Relations Association of America.

---

1. T. G. Spates, "Analysis of Industrial Relations Trend" (Conference of the Labor College at Philadelphia); American Management Association, Personnel Series No. 25 (1929), p. 12.

The year 1922 saw the merger of the National Association of
Corporation Training with the Industrial Relations Association of
America into the National Personnel Association. A year later the
new organisation changed its name to the American Management Association. In 1925 it was greatly strengthened when the National Association of Sales Managers joined the group. The development falls into
three movements:

      1. Employment Management.
      2. Personnel Management.
      3. Management.

The movements of the Corporation Schools and Employment Management
were contemporaneous and were followed by the Personal Management phase,
and later by Management. At a Board Meeting of February 16, 1927, the
object of the American Management was stated as follows:

> "To advance the understanding of the principles,
> policies, and practices of modern management; and ad-
> ministration and methods of creating and maintaining
> satisfactory human relations in commerce and industry."[1]

The Association does this through regular meetings and the publication of papers presented before these meetings. The papers are printed
in any one of the six series, to wit:

      1. Proceedings of the Institute of Management.
      2. General Management Series.
      3. Personnel Series.
      4. Production Executive Series.
      5. Office Management Series, or
      6. As Special Papers.

---

1. See further on the American Management Association: W. H. Lange,
"The American Management Association and Its Predecessors,"
(Industrial Relations Counselors, Inc.), New York, 1928, Special
Paper No. 17.

These associations and institutions are all mediums for the sharing of knowledge acquired in the practical application of scientific management principles. Like colleges and universities, they are serving two main purposes: First, the accumulation of data and the building of a store of knowledge which forms the cornerstone of professional management, and second, they form the distribution centers for the sharing of the accumulated knowledge.

They aid in the building of libraries on management, sifting that which is being written and published. They are in a position to obtain the latest information on new developments directly from business. Furthermore, they are also in a position to organise new courses, lectures, study circles, conferences, etc.

There are other organisations whose work is also important. The management movement has come to the point where management consultants occupy practically the same position in the management field as the C.P.A. holds in his field.

International Management Movement.

During the period before the World War, especially in the beginning of the Twentieth Century, the rapid strides made by American industry caused the industrial world to turn to the United States and inquire into the reasons for these rapid advancements. This explains the many translations into foreign languages of such management classics as the papers of Taylor, Gantt and the writings of Gilbreth and others. It is, for instance, a well-known fact that the publications of Gilbreth on time and motion studies and on fatigue studies have generally received more attention and are more widely read in European countries than in the United States.

The diffusion of scientific management methods was to a great extent brought about through persons who were in direct touch with Taylor, had read his books and knew of his experiments; such men as Le Chatellier and Freminville in France, the Belgian employer, Bollinkx, and the Finnish professor Sederholm.

Some confusion resulted in Europe when the opposition to "Taylorism" in the United States became known, but it did not prevent a further diffusion of scientific management principles. Opposition gained ground in France for similar reasons as that in the United States, i.e., because of a too hasty introduction of scientific management methods with complete disregard for the necessary preliminary steps. Since the War, more rapid progress has been made. In Germany, education in scientific management principles has largely been concentrated around the educational institutions such as technical and commercial "Hochschulen." In France, it has been the Centre d'Étude administratives, founded by Fayol, which has given special attention to technical research; scientific management principles and methods are also taught in the schools of mines and civil engineering.

In general, education in scientific management in European countries is given by universities, colleges and special technical schools. In England, Switzerland, Holland, Czechoslovakia and other countries, the higher technical schools are giving education in scientific management. In Belgium, courses in scientific management are supplied by the Institute Solvay at Brussels, and at the Ecole du Travail at Charleroi, In Germany and England, classes are held on the basis of direct relations to actual industrial life.

For more practical studies in scientific management, trade associations are playing a leading role in France, Germany, Czechoslovakia, Great

Britain, Finland, Switzerland, Poland and Russia. In Russia, there exists a Central Scientific Management Council (Sovnot). The most specialized institution in Russia is the Central Labor Institute at Moscow, but this country had as many as sixty local institutions throughout the territory of the Union by 1924, some of them even in districts like Turkestan, the Caucasus, and Siberia. All these local institutions carry on research as well as educational and publicity work.

The World War period and thereafter showed the universal need of modernizing methods of factory management and administration. This movement became a regular school of thought, the "doctrine administrative," in France founded by Henri Fayol. He made a definite contribution to the scientific management movement by stressing new functions which he called "administrative functions." These functions included forecasting, organization, direction, coordination, and supervision. Fayolism does not oppose Taylorism. Taylor was more concerned with the inner organization of the shop while Fayol called attention to the principle of unified direction and was more concerned with the harmonious working of the several departments of a large industrial enterprise. That there is no antagonism between the two systems was indicated by the presence of Henri Fayol at the International Congress on Scientific Management in Brussels in 1925.

Attention should also be called to two special developments in the scientific management movement abroad. The first is in regard to Czechoslovakia in which country the movement has a definitely political aspect. All institutions are affiliated with a single body, the Masaryk Labor Academy in Prague. The government gives effective support to the movement since political independence is strongly connected with economic

independence. Economic independence in turn is sought through the
introduction of improved industrial methods.

Another rather interesting development is going on in Finland.
In this country the scientific management movement has a most characteristic
feature in that scientific management principles are applied to agriculture,
and have especially been applied to plowing. In 1925, the Finnish Society
for Scientific Management in Agriculture was founded and now makes studies
for the improvement in agricultural methods.

The international scientific management congress held at Prague
in 1924 had been carefully prepared by the Masaryk Labor Academy. It
was attended by leading American scientific management men, among them
Mr. and Mrs. Gilbreth who represented the Taylor Society and the American
Engineering Council. Much time was given to a general account on the
state of scientific management in the United States and steps taken by
Russia toward more efficient working methods and for increasing industrial
output.

The Prague Congress brought into being the International Committee
for Scientific Management which was first sponsored by Czechoslovakia,
Yugoslavia, Poland and Rumania. In 1927, Belgium, Bulgaria, France,
Italy, Spain and the United States became parties to this committee. The
purposes of this Committee are:

> "(1) To decide every second year in what country the next
> congress will be held and to link up the various con-
> gresses.
>
> "(2) To organize the exchange of information between the
> different national committees and to be the moving
> spirit in this exchange.
>
> "(3) To publish a quarterly periodical which will ensure
> the diffusion of general information of an inter-
> national character."[1]

---

1. Paul Devinat, Scientific Management in Europe, (International Labor
   Office, Studies and Reports), Geneva, 1927, p. 224.

The International Management Institute was founded by a decision of representatives of the Boston Twentieth Century Fund, the International Labor Office and the International Committee for Scientific Management. Membership is open to any government, institution for public service, trade association or union, as well as to any group of governments, institutions for public service or trade associations. The seat of the Institute is in Geneva. Its purpose is to further the development of scientific management methods and to lend it practical and disinterested support, to coordinate the work of research, education and application heretofore carried out in the different countries, and to assure a free exchange of information and documents between all those engaged in production and distribution. Its object therefore is to collect and distribute information concerning management in its various aspects, to carry on research and surveys bearing on the problems of management, to bring persons and institutions specially interested in the problems of the scientific organization of production and distribution into contact with one another, and to assist appropriate national and international institutions in their work in the interest of scientific management.

The science of medicine has been in the course of development throughout many centuries and, as the body of scientifically determined laws and principles relating to the subject has grown and obtained more wider acceptance, it has become increasingly necessary to rigidly control the application of this knowledge. The welfare of society and the integrity of social institutions have demanded that only those persons be admitted to the practice of this science whose qualifications and personal fitness to assume the responsibilities involved could be clearly demonstrated. From many points of view, the application of the laws and principles of

management to the activities of enterprise affects with equal seriousness
the welfare of the people and their institutions. Thus it is pertinent
to observe that as the principles and laws of management develop, as did
those of medicine, the tendency will become more evident to protect the
welfare of the people through controlling those who apply these laws and
principles. There is a significant trend in existence today which bears
directly upon the considerations here involved. The proposal is advanced
in many quarters that enterprise exists only as it serves the welfare of
the people and that the function of management and ownership is that of
trusteeship. It is argued that this trusteeship has its accountability
to society at large rather than to legal ownership in particular. The
acceptance of this philosophy would quickly and strongly emphasize the
necessity for delegating this public trust to those persons only who
could qualify according to the standards approved by society just as is
now the practice with respect to those activities which constitute government in the interests of public welfare. This thesis is not defended here
and the philosophy mentioned may not eventuate into practice. There are,
however, so many collateral implications attached to the application of
the art and science of management which find their way into every stratum
of human activity that whether or not the theory of social trusteeship
becomes the guiding motive of our economy, the need for the better control
of the agencies upon which our welfare depends is steadily growing and
finding expression. An evidence of this is suggested by the National
Labor Relations Board which has as its primary objective the development
and preservation of the most beneficial relationships between owner and
worker. The Securities and Exchange Commission and the Fair Labor
Standards Administration are but an illustration of other agencies designed
for similar purposes. It is generally believed that the failure on the

part of enterprise to conduct its affairs in such manner as to provide the maximum of social benefits has led to the introduction of these legal agencies. This could easily imply that there has been a pronounced failure on the part of enterprises to apply sincerely and effectively the known laws and principles of management in such a way as would result in the greatest good for society. An analogy of this is the laws which become operative immediately a person endowed with the privilege of practicing medicine betrays his trust. This comparison could be expanded to show similar lines of development and action in various other fields but the case appears to be entirely clear without this additional evidence. The following chapter will undertake to crystallize the analysis of the data presented in this and preceding chapters in the form of conclusions and deductions in an effort to show to what extent, if at all, management is moving toward professional status.

CHAPTER VI
CONCLUSIONS

In every era throughout recorded history, there have been a few people capable of examining from a detached viewpoint and with clear perspective the more important aspects of national life and of focusing the attention of others upon the problems and the areas in which improvement could be made.

The trend toward the professionalization of management is a development which has occurred largely during the twentieth century although its beginnings are rooted in the fundamental changes that took place during the three closing decades of the nineteenth century. The era of business consolidation that budded in the eighties, and flowered in the nineties, culminated shortly after the turn of the century as a result of the so-called "trust busting" activities of President Theodore Roosevelt. The counterpart of this period got under way in the middle twenties.

According to a statement made by the President of Colgate-Palmolive-Peet Company before a gathering of New York University students in May of 1924:"it was necessary for the national good to so combine business as to take advantage of the limited amount of properly trained and experienced management." Although the efforts of President Theodore Roosevelt as well as the efforts of recent Federal administrations to abolish big business have been unsuccessful, they have served the purpose of emphasizing the fact that in order for large-scale enterprise to survive, it must conduct its activities with such efficiency and benefit to the public as to merit and receive public support. Leaders in education, business and government recognize many other factors, conditions, and developments, which are serving to emphasize this growing need for trained and skilled leaders. Some of these factors and conditions are:

1. The increasing complexity and extent of business activities and trade relationships.

2. The increasingly rapid development and expansion of technology and mechanization.

3. The increasingly wide use of the corporate form of organization and its concomitants.

4. The rapid growth and increasingly widespread activities of organized labor.

5. The increasing extent of restrictive regulatory legislation imposed by the states and the federal government.

6. The shrinking margins of profits caused by increased taxation and legislative minimum wages and maximum hours of work.

7. The plentitude and ready availability of capital for new enterprise.

8. The keener interest in and greater necessity for self-sufficiency from the viewpoint of national defense.

9. The increasingly great public concern over waste of resources and the rapid diminution of the supply of available natural resources.

10. A wide range of undesirable and correctable social conditions.

11. The rapid development and expansion of transportation
    and communication facilities and their effects upon
    industry, commerce, government, and social development.

These evidences are sufficient to demonstrate the point that
great pressure exists on every side to bring about the improvement of
management methods and practices in American business. Mr. Allan Mogensen,
a nationally known consultant in management, said in an address before
the National Office Management Association on April 18, 1939, "there is
so much avoidable waste in American business that its cost equals the
sum needed to raise the annual income of every American worker from its
present level to $2500 per annum,and this waste is attributable in my
judgment and from my investigations in hundreds of leading business concerns to management failures." In 1924, Mr. Herbert Hoover, then Secretary
of the Department of Commerce of the Federal government, said, "American
business is approximately sixty per cent efficient in its operation and
of this forty per cent inefficiency, eighty-five per cent is attributable
to management." Again, in 1910, the statement was made by Justice Louis D.
Brandeis in the eastern railroad rate case that the "application of
proper management practices to the operation of American railroads would
produce a savings of more than one million dollars daily." The testimony given above, clearly demonstrates the need for better management in
American enterprise. The question that logically arises next is, how can
this needed improvement be accomplished? The writer believes,as do most
students of the subject, that the one certain way in which this improvement
can be achieved is through the development of professional management. By
granting to and demanding of those who manage, the essential qualities char-
acterizing other professions, the practices, methods. standards, ethics, and
knowledge of the subject, and its practice can be improved to a very great

degree, if the improvements resulting from the achievement of professional status of other fields is a reliable criterion. Leading authorities accept the statement that the quality of management is improving, but they argue that the improvement is coming altogether too slowly and at too great a cost. When the Institute of Management was formed and formally dedicated on December 4, 1939 by its founder Harry Arthur Hopf, one of the leading authorities on management in the world, he said, "It is the hope of the co-founders and myself that the launching of the Hopf Institute of Management will be not only a means of training more men for the profession of management, but that it will also act as a challenge to those now engaged in such training and thereby accelerate the pace in order that the fruits of abundance may become available to our entire people at a much earlier period."

It is not difficult to criticise and find fault with the methods that have and to some extent are presently being used in training managers, but it is difficult to submit a constructive program of training that will hasten the day when American enterprise can operate at optimum rates. This subject would be material for further research, and it offers a field of great potential value to business and education.

The challenge of this research study is not to evaluate the current methods of training managers, however, but rather to evaluate such trends as may be discernible which will indicate to any degree or which will oppose the premise that management is moving toward a professional status. The preceding chapters of this study are devoted to the discussion of the historical developments and fundamental changes that have been taking place in our economy since 1860, in order to delineate or to show the lack of such trends. Through the application of the established criteria, it has become possible to identify certain trends which

are considered to be significant in this connection. Among the primary
trends which appear to be in evidence to support the belief that management is moving toward professional status may be mentioned:

1. The founding of the Wharton School of Finance of the
   University of Pennsylvania in 1881, the School of Commerce,
   Accounts, and Finance of New York University in 1900, and
   the subsequent establishment of schools of business administration by leading universities throughout the
   country and the establishment by these universities
   of graduate schools of business.

2. The establishment by such large industrial concerns
   as the General Motors Corporation, the United States
   Steel Corporation and others of institutes for the
   training of technicians and managers.

3. The inauguration since 1900 by many leading industrial
   concerns of extensive training programs covering periods
   of from a few months to several years (as in the case of
   the Goodrich Rubber Company, the A. T. and T. Company,
   R. H. Macy and Company, and many others) for the purpose
   of training executives in specialized fields of management and for general management work.

4. The development since 1900 of many consulting management
   firms.

5. The development of the American Society of Mechanical
   Engineers in 1883 and the subsequent development of more
   than one hundred societies and associations whose objective
   is the development, exchange, and dissemination of facts,
   practices, and data relating to management and the problems

of enterprise.

6. The promotion by religious and social institutions and by municipal governments of training programs for the development of new managers and for the improvement of those already engaged in management work.

7. The passage of legislation in various states requiring certification on the basis of specified qualifications of those intending to practise in various fields of management, such as certified accounting, technical engineering, and industrial engineering.

8. The practice followed by several associations in setting up standards of qualifications for persons intending to practise in that particular branch of management. Examples of this are to be found in the standard set by the Comptrollers Institute of America and the National Office Management Association.

9. The close cooperation of various associations such as the Comptrollers Institute of America, the American Marketing Association, the National Office Management Association, and the Federation of Sales Executives of America with colleges and graduate schools of business to bring about the introduction of specific courses into the curriculum as a basic training for persons intending to practise in these specialized fields of management.

10. A rapidly crystallising social consciousness of management's responsibilities to the public as of primary importance and its responsibility to the employer as of secondary importance (this point of view is reflected in many of the

recent textbooks on industrial management, personnel
management, human relations, and social control).

11. The increasingly widespread use of the corporate form of
legal organization. (This produces a widespread and
impersonal quality of ownership which is one of the great
influences in promoting an opportunity for trained and
paid management to conduct the affairs of business for
its owners.)

12. The growing size of the business unit and the concomitant
that the increasingly diversified interests of the business and its owners makes necessary the utilization of
paid managers to supplement the abilities and to assume
a portion of the responsibilities required of the owners.

13. The tendency on the part of corporation boards of directors
to delegate more and more of the operating responsibilities
of business to paid management. (This tendency was stated
by Mr. W. R. Donaldson, president of the Robert Gair Company,
in an address before the Management Club of New York University in 1937. It was reiterated by Mr. W. R. Fuller, president of the Curtis Publishing Company at a luncheon meeting
of the Office Management Division of the American Management
Association on October 6, 1938. It was stated in even
stronger terms by Mr. Thomas Roy Jones, president of American
Type Founders Company in an article entitled, "Dog Fights
and Organization Charts" which appeared in the December 1938
issue of Dun's review).

14. The development of an International Management Institute
(with headquarters at Geneva, Switzerland) for the purpose

of bringing about a better understanding through an interchange of management knowledge and data between business
leaders of the world. In this connection, seven international management congresses have been held in various
parts of the world to promote the development of general
and specialized management. The most recent congress was
held in September of 1938 in Washington, D. C.

15. The rapid growth of reference and textbooks on general
and specialized management.

16. The number of periodicals relating to general or
specific management fields and the size of their circu-
lation.

17. The utilization by the Federal government of existing
governmental organizations and the creation of new
ones for cooperation with business leaders and for
the dissemination of valuable information relating
to training, placement, job specifications, standards,
management principles, and documentary material.

18. The passage of various legislative enactments by the
several states and the federal government which indirectly affect the quality of management through
exacting penalties for failures on the part of management. The Workmen's Compensation Act is a characteristic illustration. In this act, management is not required to conform to given standards but if management
fails to establish standards and conform to them and
such a failure causes injury to a workman, the business

must assume the responsibility for a damage award which
will be made by the state.

The application of the criteria used throughout this study does
not disclose any definite trends that would negate the statement that
there is a definite evidence of a trend toward the professionalization
of management. It is that in the course of economic change and s. al
adjustment, certain temporary conditions develop which might be interpreted as opposed to the trend already mentioned. These conditions
are so patently temporary, however, that it is considered justifiable
to ignore them. There are on the business horizon today many vague
and indefinite signs of new movement which may or may not materialize.
It would not be scientific to speculate as to their content at this
time. Therefore, they, too, have been ignored.

Although the evidence herein marshalled does substantiate the
current opinion among business and educational leaders that management
is moving toward professional status, it by no means definitely establishes the fact beyond peradventure. It will be necessary for those
interested in this uestion to constantly study the impact of changes,
developments, and counter-movements, and to interpret them in the
light of the criteria already established as a means of following
whatever direction the current trend may take. The subject is one that
should be of interest to most people, inasmuch as the development of
professional management augurs well for an enduring and substantial
improvement in our social and economic welfare.

BIBLIOGRAPHY

A. Books

Alford, L. P., Henry Laurance Gantt Leader in Industry. New York and London: Harper and Brothers, 1934.

Alford, L. P., Principles of Industrial Management for Engineers. New York: The Ronald Press, 1940.

Babbage, Charles, On The Economy of Machinery and Manufactures. London: Charles Knight, 1832.

Babcock, George D., The Taylor System in Franklin Management, in collaboration with Reginald Trautschold and with a Foreword by Carl G. Barth, (Industrial Management Library, the Engineering Magazine Company) New York, 1917.

Bemis, E. W., History of Cooperation in the United States, (Johns Hopkins University Historical and Political Studies, Vol. 6) Baltimore, 1888. See part on "Cooperation in New England".

Boehmert, Victor, "Die Gewinnbeteiligung" Untersuchungen ueber Arbeitslohn und Unternehmergewinn, Two volumes. Leipzig: F. A. Brockhaus, 1878.

Brandeis, Louis D., Business A Profession. Boston: Small, Maynard and Company, 1914.

Brandeis, Louis D., Scientific Management and the Railroads, being part of a brief submitted to the Interstate Commerce Commission, (The Engineering Magazine) New York, 1912.

Burton, E. R., Employee Representation, with a Foreword by Henry Metcalf. Baltimore: The Williams and Wilkins Company, 1926.

Copley, Frank Barkley, Frederick W. Taylor, Father of Scientific Management. New York and London: Harper and Brothers, 1923, (Two volumes).

Cornell, W. B., Organization and Management in Industry and Business. New York: The Ronald Press Company, 1936.

Dartmouth College, Scientific Management, Addresses and Discussions held at the Tuck School Conference on Scientific Management, October 12, 13, 14, 1911. Dartmouth College, Hanover, N. H., 1912.

Devinat, Paul, Scientific Management in Europe. (International Labor Office, Studies and Reports) Geneva, 1927.

Diemer, H., Factory Organization and Administration. New York:
McGraw-Hill Book Company, 1935.

Drury, Horace Bookwalter, Scientific Management. A History and
Criticism. (Columbia University Studies in History,
Economics and Public Law; Faculty of Political Science)
New York, 1922 (Revised and enlarged edition).

Emerson, H., The Twelve Principles of Efficiency. (The Engineering
Magazine Company) New York, 1922.

Fawcett, Henry, Pauperism: Its Causes and Remedies. London and
New York: Macmillan and Company, 1871.

Fayol, Henri, Industrial and General Administration. London:
Sir Isaac Pitman and Sons, Ltd., 1930.

Federated American Engineering Societies, Waste in Industry,
Report of the Committee on Elimination of Waste in Industry.
New York: McGraw-Hill Book Company, 1921.

Frommer, Heinrich, Die Gewinnbeteilligung. ihre praktische Anwendung
and Theoretische Berechtigung of Grund Bisherigen Erfahrungen.
Leipzig: Verlag von Dunker und Humbolt, 1887.

Gantt, Henry Laurence, Industrial Leadership, Addresses delivered in
the Page Lecture Series in 1915, before the Senior Class of
the Sheffield Scientific School, Yale University. New Haven:
Yale University Press, 1916.

Gantt, Henry Laurence, Organizing for Work. New York: Harcourt,
Brace and Howe, 1919.

Gantt, Henry Laurence, Work, Wages, and Profits. (The Engineering
Magazine Company) New York, 1919, (Second and enlarged edition,
first printed in 1913).

Gerstenberg, C. W., Financial Organization and Management of Business.
New York: Prentice-Hall, Inc., 1932.

Gilbreth, Frank L. and Lillian Moller, Applied Motion Study.
New York: Sturgis and Walton, 1917.

Gilbreth, Frank L., Fatigue Study. New York: The Macmillan Company,
1919.

Gilman, N. P., Profit Sharing Between Employers and Employees.
Boston and New York: Houghton, Mifflin and Company, 1889.

Hoxie, Robert Franklin, Scientific Management and Labor. New York
and London: D. Appleton and Company, 1915.

Hunt, E. E., Influence of Scientific Management, in the Taylor
Society publication of Scientific Management in American
Industry. (The Taylor Society) New York, 1929.

Hunt, E. E., _Scientific Management Since Taylor_. New York:
McGraw Hill Book Company, 1924.

Jones, E. D., _The Administration of Industrial Enterprises_.
New York, London, and Toronto: Longsman, Green and Company,
1932.

Lichtner, W. O., _Planned Control in Manufacturing_. New York:
The Ronald Press, 1924.

Massachusetts Bureau of Labor Statistics, "_Seventeenth Annual
Report_.

Metcalf, Henry C., _Business Leadership_. New York and London:
Isaac Pitman and Sons, 1930.

Metcalf, Henry C., (ed.) _Business Management As A Profession_.
Chicago: A. W. Show Company, 1927.

National Industrial Conference Board, _Financial Incentives_.
New York City: No. 217, 1935.

National Industrial Conference Board, _Industrial Relations:
Administration of Policies and Programs_. New York, 1931

Person, Harlow Stafford, _Industrial Education: a System of
Training for Men Entering Upon Trade and Commerce_. Boston
and New York: Houghton, Mifflin and Company, 1907.

President's Conference on Unemployment, Report of the Committee
on Recent Economic Changes, "Recent Economic Changes in the
United States". New York: McGraw Hill Book Company, 1929.
(Four volumes).

President's Research Committee on Social Trends, _Recent Social
Trends in the United States_. New York: McGraw-Hill Book
Company, 1933.

Princeton University, Industrial Relations Section, _Corporation
Training Programs_. Princeton, New Jersey.

Robert, Charles, _La Suppression des Grèves par L'Association aux
Benefices_ (conference faite a la Sorbonne le 27 Decembre 1869)
Librairie Hachette et Cie, Paris 1870.

Schulze, John William, _The American Office: Its Organization,
Management, and Records_. New York: Key Publishing Company, 1913.

Sheldon, Oliver, _The Philosophy of Management_. New York: Prentice-
Hall, Inc., 1924.

Smith, Adam, _An Inquiry into the Nature and Causes of the Wealth of
Nations_. Edinburgh: Adam and Charles Black, 1855. (Fourth
edition).

Spencer, Herbert, _The Study of Sociology_. New York: D. Appleton
and Company, 1880.

Taylor, Frederick W., _On The Art of Cutting Metals_. (American
Society of Mechanical Engineers) New York, 1906.

Taylor, Frederick W., _The Principles of Scientific Management_.
New York and London: Harper and Brothers, 1917.

Taylor, Frederick W., _Shop Management_, with an introduction by
Henry R. Towne. Norwood, Massachusetts: The Plimpton
Press, 1911.

Taylor Society, New York, _Scientific Management in American
Industry_. New York: Harper Brothers, 1929.

Tead, Ordway, _The Art of Leadership_. New York: McGraw-Hill Book
Company, 1935.

United States Labor Bureau, _First Annual Report_. (Government
Printing Office) Washington, D. C., 1886.

United States Census of Manufacturers (Government Printing Office)
Washington, D. C. ...

B. Periodicals, Pamphlets and Technical Papers.

Alford, L. P., _Ten Years Progress in Management_, (Transactions of
the American Society of Mechanical Engineers, pp. 1243-1296)
New York, 1922.

American Institute of Consulting Engineers, _Petition of Professional
Engineers to the Senate and Assembly of the State of New York_.
March 21, 1921. (In support of Senate Bill No. 147,716 for
professional licensing.)

Balderston, C. C., _The Technique of Basing Extra Compensation of
Managers and Executives on Profits_, a gross section of
current practice with pre-determined profit-sharing. (American Management Association, General Management Series No. 84)
New York, 1929.

Barber, Joseph H., _Coordination of Sales and Production at the
Walworth Manufacturing Company_. (Bulletin of the Taylor
Society, Vol. IX. No. 3) New York, 1924.

Barth, Carl G., _Slide Rule of the Machine Shop as a Part of the
Taylor System of Management_. (Transactions of the American
Society of Mechanical Engineers, Vol. XXV, pp. 49-62) New
York, 1904.

Bergen, Harold B., and Bergen, Garret Lawrence, _Executive Training
Programs_. (American Management Association, General Management Series No. 107) New York, 1929.

Black, John B., Folsom, M. B. and Others, _Practical Aspect of Unemployment Insurance and Old Age Security_. (American Management
Association, Personnel Series No. 23) New York, 1936.

Brown, Geoffrey C., _Scientific Management and Organized Labor Today_.
(Bulletin of the Taylor Society, Vol. X, No. 3) New York, 1925.

Browne, H. V., Recent Office Economies. (American Management
Association, Office Management Series No. 56) New York,
1932.

Cooke, Morris Llewellyn, The Influence of Scientific Management
Upon Government--Federal, State and Municipal. (Bulletin of
the Taylor Society, Vol. XI, No. 1) New York, 1924.

Cooke, Morris Llewellyn, Who is Boss in Your Shop? (Annals of
the American Academy of Political and Social Science, Vol. 71)
New York, 1917. (pp. 167-185).

Coonly, Howard, The Control of an Industry in the Business Cycles.
(Harvard Business Review, Vol. 1, No. 4) Cambridge, Mass.,
1923.

Copley, Frank Barkley, Frederick W. Taylor, Revolutionist,
privately printed with special permission from the Outlook
of September 1, 1915 (The Plimpton Press) Norwood, Massachusetts, 1916.

DuBrul, E. E., The Machine Tool Industry's Code of Business
Principles. (American Management Association, General Management Series No. 78) New York, 1928.

Eastman, Lucius R., The Future of the Business Man. (American
Management Association, Annual Convention Series, No. 12)
New York, 1925.

Ellerd, Harvey C., Rating Supervisors. (American Management
Association, Production Executive Series No. 42) New York,
1929.

Feiss, Richard A., Personal Relationship as a Basis for Scientific
Management. (Bulletin of the Taylor Society, Vol. 1, No. 6)
New York, 1915.

Feiss, Richard A., The Spirit of Scientific Management. (Abstract
of an address delivered before the Annual Convention of the
National Association of Clothiers and of the Annual Convention
of the National Boot and Shoe Manufacturers Association) New
York, 1917.

Fuller, Walter B., Application of Scientific Management Principles
to Office Management. (Bulletin of the Taylor Society, Vol. 4,
No. 5) New York, 1919.

Gantt, Henry Laurence, A Bonus System of Rewarding Labor. (Transactions of the American Society of Mechanical Engineers,
Vol. XXIII, pp. 341 and following) New York, 1901.

Gantt, Henry Laurence, A Graphical Daily Balance in Manufacture.
(Transactions of the American Society of Mechanical Engineers,
Vol. XXIV, pp. 1322 and following) New York, 1903.

Gantt, Henry Laurence, A Modifying System of Management. (Transactions of the American Society of Mechanical Engineers, Vol. XXV, pp. 65-67) New York, 1904.

Gilbreth, Frank L. and Lillian Moller, Stop Watch Time Study: An Indictment and Defense, a symposium in which Carl G. Barth, Dwight V. Merrick and Others took part, (Bulletin of the Taylor Society, Vol. VI, No. 3) New York, 1921.

Gilbreth, Frank L., Super Standards. (Bulletin of the Taylor Society, Vol. VII, No. 3) New York, 1922.

Green, William, Labor's Ideals Concerning Management. (Bulletin of the Taylor Society, Vol. X, No. 6) New York, 1925.

Halsey, F. A., A Premium Plan of Paying Labor. (Transactions of the American Society of Mechanical Engineers, pp. 755 and following) New York, 1891.

Hoover, Herbert, Industrial Waste. (Bulletin of the Taylor Society, Vol. 6, No. 2) New York, 1921.

Kendall, Henry P., The Problem of the Chief Executive. (Bulletin of the Taylor Society, Vol. 7, No. 2) New York, 1922.

Kent, William, A Problem in Profit Sharing. (Transactions of the American Society of Mechanical Engineers, Vol. 8, pp. 632-633) New York, 1887

Leffingwell, Henry Wm., The Application of Principles of Scientific Management to the Office. (Bulletin of the Taylor Society, Vol. 7, No. 1) New York, 1922.

Lichtner, William O., Promulgation of Standards by the Taylor Society. (Bulletin of the Taylor Society, Vol. 5, No. 4) New York, 1920.

McKinsey, James O., Functions of Board of Directors, Board Committees and Officers. (American Management Association, General Management Series No. 82) New York, 1929.

Miller, Justin, The Philosophy of Professional Licensure, an address delivered at the Thirtieth Annual Congress on Medical Education, Licensure and Hospitals in Chicago, February 12, 1934, (National Council of State Boards of Engineering Examiners) Columbia, S. C., 1937.

Otterson, J. E., Executive and Administrative Organization. (The Annals of the American Academy of Political and Social Science, Vol. 85, pp. 90-99) New York, 1919.

Person, Harlow Stafford, The Contribution of Scientific Management to Industrial Problems. (Bulletin of the Taylor Society, Vol. VIII, No. 3) New York, 1923.

Proceedings of the Conference at Chicago, Employees Representation Technique. (American Management Association, Production Executive Series, No. 49) New York, 1926.

228

Report on the Organisation and Function of the Sales Engineering
Department. (Bulletin of the Taylor Society, Vol. 5, No. 6)
New York, 1920.

Rich, R. B., Principles of Wage Payment. (Bulletin of the Taylor
Society, Vol. XI, No. 4) New York, 1926.

Richards, Frank, A Gift Proposition for Paying Workmen. (Transactions of the American Society of Mechanical Engineers,
Vol. XXIV, pp. 250 and following) New York, 1903.

Shaw, Albert, Cooperation in a Western City, in Vol. 1, No. 4 of
the publication of the American Economic Association, 188.

Spates, T. G., Industrial Relations Trend, with sub-title, An
Analysis of Industrial Relations Trend. (American Management
Association, Personnel Series, No. 25) New York, 1937.

Taylor, Frederick Winslow, Notes on Belting. (Transactions of the
American Society of Mechanical Engineers, Vol. XV, pp. 204-259)
New York, 1894.

Taylor, Frederick Winslow, A Piece Rate System. (Transactions of the
American Society of Mechanical Engineers, Vol. XVI, pp. 865-903)
New York, 1895.

Taylor, F. W., Shop Management. (Transactions of the American
Society of Mechanical Engineers, Vol. XXIV, pp. 1337 and following)
New York, 1903.

Taylor, F. W., Success. A lecture to young men entering business,
held before the engineering students at the University of Illinois
and the University of Cincinnati, February 1909 (Bulletin of the
Taylor Society, Vol. XI, No. 2) New York, 1926, (also available
as a reprint).

Towne, Henry R., "The Engineer as An Economist. (Transactions of the
American Society of Mechanical Engineers, Vol. VIII, pp. 427-432)
New York, 1886.

Towne, Henry R., Gain Sharing. (Transactions of the American Society
of Mechanical Engineers, Vol. X, pp. 600 and following) New York,
1889.

Urick, L., The Development of Scientific Management in Great Britain.
(British Management Review, Vol. 3, No. 4, p. 10)

Yoakum, C. S., Present Status of Management Research Methods. (American Management Association, Proceedings of the Institute, No. 4)
New York, 1928.

Vol. 2 of a "Collection de Memoires", made by the "Societe Francaise
de Physique", and published in 1884. Paris, France.

C. Documents and Records.

United States Committee on Education and Labor, Eight Hour Law,
Hearings held from January to and including March, 1912,
(United States Senate 62nd Session; House Resolution 9061)
Washington, Government Printing Office, 1912.

United States Committee on Labor, Investigation of (the) Taylor
System of Shop Management. (House of Representatives,
62nd Congress 1st Session, H. R. 90) Washington, Government
Printing Office, 1911.

United States Labor Committee, Investigation of the Taylor System
of Shop Management. (House of Representatives, 62nd Congress
2nd Session) Washington, Government Printing Office, 1911.

United States Labor Committee, Report No. 1175 on Federal Legislation on the Taylor and Other Systems of Shop Management.
(63rd Congress, 2nd Session, House of Representatives,
Report No. 1175, serial 6560) Washington, Government
Printing Office, 1914.

United States Commission on Industrial Relations, Final Report
and Testimony Submitted to Congress... (64th Congress, 1st
Session, Senate Document No. 415) created by the Act of
August 23, 1912. Washington, Government Printing Office,
1915 (Ten volumes).

United States Senate, Evidence Taken by the Interstate Commerce
Commission in the Matter of Proposed Advances in Freight
Rates by Carriers. (United States Senate, 61st Congress,
3rd Session, Senate Document No. 725) August to December
1910. Washington Government Printing Office, 1912. (Ten
volumes).

United States, Special Committee of the House of Representatives
to Investigate the Taylor System of Shop Management. (Under
authority of House Resolution 90) Washington Government
Printing Office, 1912. (Vol. 8, pp. 1265-1938).

COMPANIES AND MEN

Business Enterprise in America

An Arno Press Collection

Allen, Hugh. **The House of Goodyear:** A Story of Rubber and of Modern Business. 1943

Bennett, Howard F. **Precision Power:** The First Half Century of Bodine Electric Company. 1959

Broehl, Wayne G., Jr. **Precision Valley:** The Machine Tool Companies of Springfield, Vermont. 1959

Broehl, Wayne G., Jr. **Trucks, Trouble and Triumph:** The Norwalk Truck Line Company. 1954

Bruchey, Eleanor S. **The Business Elite in Baltimore, 1880-1914.** 1976

Burgess, George H. and Miles C. Kennedy. **Centennial History of the Pennsylvania Railroad Company, 1846-1946.** 1949

Cleland, David Ira. **The Origin and Development of a Philosophy of Long-Range Planning in American Business.** 1976

Darr, Richard K. **A History of the Nashua and Lowell Rail-Road Corporation, 1835-1880.** 1976

Engelbourg, Saul. **International Business Machines:** A Business History. 1976

Gibb, George Sweet. **The Whitesmiths of Taunton:** A History of Reed & Barton, 1824-1943. 1943

Gibb, George Sweet and Evelyn H. Knowlton. **History of Standard Oil Company (New Jersey): The Resurgent Years, 1911-1927.** 1956

Giddens, Paul H. **Standard Oil Company (Indiana): Oil Pioneer of the Middle West.** 1955

Gloster, Jesse Edward. **North Carolina Mutual Life Insurance Company.** 1976

Gras, N[orman] S. B. **The Massachusetts First National Bank of Boston, 1784-1934.** 1937

Hidy, Ralph W. and Muriel E. Hidy. **History of Standard Oil Company (New Jersey): Pioneering in Big Business, 1882-1911.** 1955

Holbert, Hayward Janes. **A History of Professional Management in American Industry.** 1976

Hungerford, Edward. **Men and Iron:** The History of New York Central. 1938

James, Marquis. **Biography of a Business, 1792-1942:** Insurance Company of North America. 1942

James, Marquis. **The Metropolitan Life:** A Study in Business Growth. 1947

Kaufman, Charles N. **The History of the Keller Manufacturing Company.** 1976

Kuniansky, Harry Richard. **A Business History of Atlantic Steel Company, 1901-1968.** 1976

Larson, Henrietta M. and Kenneth Wiggins Porter. **History of Humble Oil & Refining Company:** A Study in Industrial Growth. 1959

Loth, David. **Swope of G.E.:** The Story of Gerard Swope and General Electric in American Business. 1958

Marcosson, Isaac F. **Anaconda.** 1957

Morison, Samuel Eliot. **The Ropemakers of Plymouth:** A History of the Plymouth Cordage Company, 1824-1949. 1950

Myers, Kenneth Holston. **Marketing Policy Determination by a Major Firm in a Capital Goods Industry:** A Case Study of Bucyrus-Erie Company, 1880-1954. 1976

Nevins, Allan. **History of the Bank of New York and Trust Company, 1784-1934.** 1934

Nevins, Allan and Frank Ernest Hill. **FORD:** Volume I, The Times, the Man, the Company; Volume II, Expansion and Challenge, 1915-1933; Volume III, Decline and Rebirth, 1933-1962. Three vols. 1954/1957/1963

Payne, Peter Lester and Lance Edwin Davis. **The Savings Bank of Baltimore, 1818-1866:** A Historical and Analytical Study. 1956

Plavchan, Ronald J. **A History of Anheuser-Busch, 1852-1933.** 1976

Puth, Robert C[hristian]. **Supreme Life:** The History of a Negro Life Insurance Company. 1976

Sanderlin, Walter S. **The Great National Project:** A History of the Chesapeake and Ohio Canal. 1946

Schwarzman, Richard C. **The Pinal Dome Oil Company:** An Adventure in Business, 1901-1917. 1976

Thomas, Norman F. **Minneapolis-Moline:** A History of Its Formation and Operations. 1976

Twyman, Robert W. **History of Marshall Field & Co., 1852-1906.** 1954

Wainwright, Nicholas B. **History of the Philadelphia National Bank:** A Century and a Half of Philadelphia Banking, 1803-1953. 1953

White, Gerald T. **Formative Years in the Far West:** A History of Standard Oil Company of California and Predecessors Through 1919. 1962

Williamson, Harold F. and Orange A. Smalley. **Northwestern Mutual Life:** A Century of Trusteeship. 1957